Let Us Python Solutions

Yashavant Kanetkar
Aditya Kanetkar

FIRST EDITION 2020

Copyright © BPB Publications, INDIA

ISBN : 9789389845013

LIMITS OF LIABILITY AND DISCLAIMER OF WARRANTY

Distributors:

BPB PUBLICATIONS
20, Ansari Road, Darya Ganj
New Delhi-110002
Ph: 23254990/23254991

BPB BOOK CENTRE
376 Old Lajpat Rai Market,
Delhi-110006
Ph: 23861747

MICRO MEDIA
Shop No. 5, Mahendra Chambers, 150
DN Rd. Next to Capital Cinema, V.T.
(C.S.T.) Station,
MUMBAI-400 001
Ph: 22078296/22078297

DECCAN AGENCIES
4-3-329, Bank Street,
Hyderabad-500195
Ph: 24756967/24756400

Published by Manish Jain for BPB Publications, 20, Ansari Road, Darya Ganj, New Delhi-110002 and Printed by him at Repro India Pvt Ltd, Mumbai

Dedicated to
Nalinee & Prabhakar Kanetkar...

About Yashavant Kanetkar

Through his books and Quest Video Courses on C, C++, Java, Python, Data Structures, .NET, IoT, etc. Yashavant Kanetkar has created, molded and groomed lacs of IT careers in the last three decades. Yashavant's books and Quest videos have made a significant contribution in creating top-notch IT manpower in India and abroad.

Yashavant's books are globally recognized and millions of students / professionals have benefitted from them. Yashavant's books have been translated into Hindi, Gujarati, Japanese, Korean and Chinese languages. Many of his books are published in India, USA, Japan, Singapore, Korea and China.

Yashavant is a much sought after speaker in the IT field and has conducted seminars/workshops at TedEx, IITs, IIITs, NITs and global software companies.

Yashavant has been honored with the prestigious "Distinguished Alumnus Award" by IIT Kanpur for his entrepreneurial, professional and academic excellence. This award was given to top 50 alumni of IIT Kanpur who have made significant contribution towards their profession and betterment of society in the last 50 years.

In recognition of his immense contribution to IT education in India, he has been awarded the "Best .NET Technical Contributor" and "Most Valuable Professional" awards by Microsoft for 5 successive years.

Yashavant holds a BE from VJTI Mumbai and M.Tech. from IIT Kanpur. Yashavant's current affiliations include being a Director of KICIT Pvt. Ltd. and KSET Pvt. Ltd. He can be reached at kanetkar@kicit.com or through http://www.kicit.com.

About Aditya Kanetkar

Aditya Kanetkar is currently working as a backend Software Engineer at Microsoft, Redmond, USA. He has been designing distributed systems software for the last 4 years. He has worked at multiple companies in the past, including Oracle, Redfin, Amazon and Arista Networks.

Aditya holds a Master's degree in Computer Science from Georgia Tech, Atlanta, and a Bachelor's degree in Computer Science and Engineering from IIT Guwahati. His current passion is anything remotely connected to Python, Machine Learning, Distributed Systems, Cloud Computing and C# related technologies. Aditya can be reached at aditya@kicit.com or through http://www.kicit.com.

Contents

1 Introduction to Python

[A] Answer the following:

(a) Mention 5 fields in which Python is popularly used.

Answer

- System Programming
- Game Programming
- Robotics Programming
- Rapid Prototyping
- Internet Scripting

(b) Where is event-driven programming popularly used?

Answer

Event-driven programming is primarily used for creating GUI application containing elements like windows, check, boxes, button, combo-boxes, scroll-bars, menus etc. When we interact with these GUI elements through mouse/keyboard/touch an event occurs and a function gets called to tackle that event.

(c) Why Python is called portable language?

Answer

We can create and test code on one platform and run it on any other platform. This makes Python a portable language.

(d) What is the single most important feature of different programming models discussed in this chapter?

Answer

Functional programming model - It decomposes a problem into a set of functions.

Procedural programming model - It solves a problem by implementing one statement (procedure) at a time. Thus it contains explicit steps that are executed in a specific order. It also uses functions, but these are not mathematical functions like the ones used in functional programming. Functional programming focuses on expressions, whereas Procedural programming focuses on statements.

Object-oriented programming model - It mimics the real world by creating inside the computer a mini-world of objects.

Event-driven programming model - It generates events when we interact with different GUI elements like Windows, check boxes, buttons, combo-boxes, scroll bars, menus, etc. Each event is tackled by calling an event handler function.

(e) Which of the following is not a feature of Python?
- Static typing
- Variable declaration before use
- Destruction of objects after use through destructor
- Run-time error handling through error numbers
- Library support for containers like Lists, Dictionaries, Tuples

Answer
- Static typing
- Variable declaration before use
- Destruction of objects after use through destructor
- Run-time error handling through error numbers

[B] State whether the following statements are True or False:

(a) Python is free to use and distribute.

Answer

True

(b) Same Python program can work on different OS - microprocessor combinations.

Answer

True

(c) It is possible to use C++ or Java libraries in a Python program.

Answer

True

(d) In Python type of the variable is decided based on its usage.

Answer

True

(e) Python cannot be used for building GUI applications.

Answer

False

(f) Python supports functional, procedural, object-oriented and event-driven programming models.

Answer

True

[C] Match the following:

a. Functional programming   1. GUI element based interaction
b. Event-driven programming   2. Interaction of objects
c. Procedural programming   3. Statements
d. Object-oriented programming   4. Maths-like functions

Answer

Functional programming - Maths-like Function
Event-driven programming - GUI element based interaction
Procedural programming - Statements
Object-oriented programming - Interaction of objects

[D] Fill in the blanks:

(a) Functional programming paradigm is also known as <u>Declarative</u> programming model.

(b) Procedural programming paradigm is also known as <u>Imperative</u> programming model.

(c) Python was created by <u>Guido Van Rossum</u>.

(d) Python programmers are often called <u>Pythonists or Pythonistas</u>.

2

Python Basics

[A] Answer the following:

(a) Write a program that swaps the values of variables **a** and **b**. You are not allowed to use a third variable. You are not allowed to perform arithmetic on **a** and **b**.

Program

```
# Swap values of two variables
a = 5
b = 10
a, b = b, a
print('a =' , a)
print('b =' , b)
```

Output

```
a = 10
b = 5
```

(b) Write a program that makes use of trigonometric functions available in math module.

Program

```
# Use of trigonometric functions
import math
a = math.pi / 6
print('The value of sine of pi / 6 is' , end = ' ')
print(math.sin(a))
print('The value of cosine of pi / 6 is' , end = ' ')
print(math.cos(a))
```

Output

```
The value of sine of pi / 6 is 0.49999999999999994
The value of cosine of pi / 6 is 0.8660254037844387
```

(c) Write a program that generates 5 random numbers in the range 10 to 50. Use a seed value of 6. Make a provision to change this seed value every time you execute the program by associating it with time of execution?

Program

```
# Generate random numbers
import random
import time

random.seed(6)
for i in range(5) :
   print(random.randint(10, 50))

print( )
t = int(time.time( ))
random.seed(t)
for i in range(5) :
   print(random.randint(10, 50))
```

Output

```
46
15
41
26
12

39
36
21
13
18
```

(d)　Use **trunc( )**, **floor( )** and **ceil( )** for numbers -2.8, -0.5, 0.2, 1.5 and 2.9 to understand the difference between these functions clearly.

Program

```
# Use of trunc( ), ceil( ) functions
import math
print(math.floor(-2.8))
print(math.trunc(-2.8))
print(math.ceil(-2.8))
print(math.floor(-0.5))
print(math.trunc(-0.5))
print(math.ceil(-0.5))
```

```
print(math.floor(0.2))
print(math.trunc(0.2))
print(math.ceil(0.2))
print(math.floor(1.5))
print(math.trunc(1.5))
print(math.ceil(1.5))
print(math.floor(2.9))
print(math.trunc(2.9))
print(math.ceil(2.9))
```

Output

```
-3
-2
-2
-1
0
0
0
0
1
1
1
2
2
2
3
```

(e) Assume a suitable value for Ramesh's basic salary. His dearness allowance is 40% of basic salary, and house rent allowance is 20% of basic salary. Write a program to calculate his gross salary.

Program

```
# Calculate gross salary
bs = 15000
da = float(bs * 0.4)
hra = float(bs * 0.2)
gs = bs + da + hra
print('Gross Salary:', gs)
```

Output

Gross Salary: 24000.0

(f) Assume a suitable value for distance between two cities (in km.). Write a program to convert and print this distance in meters, feet, inches and centimeters.

Program

```
# Distance calculation in different units
kms = 65
meters = int(kms * 1000)
cms = int(meters * 100)
inches = int(cms / 2.54)
feet = int(inches / 12)
print('Distance in meter:', meters, 'm')
print('Distance in feet:', feet, 'ft')
print('Distance in inches:', inches, 'inch')
print('Distance in centimeters:', cms, 'cm')
```

Output

```
Distance in meter:  65000 m
Distance in feet:  213254 ft
Distance in inches:  2559055 inch
Distance in centimeters:  6500000 cm
```

(g) Assume a suitable value for temperature of a city in Fahrenheit degrees. Write a program to convert this temperature into Centigrade degrees and print both temperatures.

Program

```
farh = 212
cen = ((farh - 32) * 5 / 9)
print(farh, cen)
```

Output

```
212 100.0
```

[B] How will you perform the following operations:

(a)   Print imaginary part out of 2 + 3j

Answer

print(a.imag)

(b)   Obtain conjugate of 4 + 2j

Answer

a = 4 + 2j
b = a.conjugate( )

(c)   Print decimal equivalent of binary '1100001110'

Answer

print(int('1100001110', 2))

(d)   Convert a float value 4.33 into a numeric string

Answer

a = str(4.33)

(e)   Obtain integer quotient and remainder while dividing 29 with 5

Answer

divmod(29, 5)

(f)   Obtain hexadecimal equivalent of decimal 34567

Answer

hex(34567)

(g)   Round-off 45.6782 to second decimal place

Answer

a = round(45.6782, 2)

(h)   Obtain 4 from 3.556

Answer

a = round(3.556)

(i)   Obtain 17 from 16.7844

Answer

a = round(16.7844)

(j)   Obtain remainder on dividing 3.45 with 1.22

Answer

a = 3.45 % 1.22

[C]   Which of the following is invalid variable name and why?

BASICSALARY - Valid

_basic - Valid

basic-hra - Invalid. Cannot contain special character -

#MEAN - Invalid. Cannot start with #

group. - Invalid. Cannot end with .

422 - Invalid. Cannot start with digit

pop in 2020 - Invalid. Cannot contain space

over - Valid

timemindovermatter - Valid

SINGLE - Valid

hELLO - Valid

queue. - Invalid. Cannot end with .

team'svictory - Invalid. Cannot contain special character '

Plot # 3 - Invalid. Cannot contain space and special character #

2015_DDay - Invalid. Cannot start with digit

[D]   Evaluate the following expressions:

(a)   2 ** 6 // 8 % 2

Answer

= 64 // 8 % 2
= 8 % 2
= 0

(b)   9 ** 2 // 5 - 3

   Answer

   = 81 // 5 - 3
   = 16 - 3
   = 13

(c)   10 + 6 - 2 % 3 + 7 - 2

   Answer

   = 10 + 6 - 2 + 7 - 2
   = 16 - 5 + 7 - 2
   = 14 + 7 - 2
   = 21 - 2
   = 19

(d)   5 % 10 + 10 -23 * 4 // 3

   Answer

   = 5 + 10 - 23 * 4 // 3
   = 5 + 10 - 92 // 3
   = 5 + 10 - 30
   = 15 - 30
   = -15

(e)   5 + 5 // 5 - 5 * 5 ** 5 % 5

   Answer

   = 5 + 5 // 5 - 5 * 3125 % 5
   = 5 + 1 - 5 * 3125 % 5
   = 5 + 1 - 15625 % 5
   = 5 + 1 - 0
   = 6

(f)   7 % 7 + 7 // 7 - 7 * 7

   Answer

   = 0 + 7 // 7 - 7 * 7
   = 0 + 1 - 7 * 7
   = 0 + 1 - 49
   = 1 - 49
   = -48

[E]   Evaluate the following expressions:

(a)   min(2, 6, 8, 5)

Answer

2

(b)   bin(46)

Answer

0b101110

(c)   round(10.544336, 2)

Answer

10.54

(d)   math.hypot(6, 8)

Answer

10

(e)   math.modf(3.1415)

Answer

0.14150000000000018, 3.0

[F]   Match the following:

a. IDLE	1. \
b. Escape special character	2. Python interactive mode
c. Extension for python script	3. Python shell prompt
d. Quickly test a Python feature	4. Script
e. Complex	5. Container type
d. Preserve program	6. py
f. Tuple	7. Basic type
g. Natural logarithm	8. log( )
h. Common logarithm	9. log10( )

Answer

IDLE - Python interactive mode
Escape special character - \
Extension for python script - py

Quickly test a python feature - Python shell prompt
Complex - Basic type
Preserve Program - Script
Tuple - Container type
Natural Logarithm - log( )
Common logarithm - log10( )

3 Strings

[A] Answer the following:

(a) Write a program that generates the following output from the string 'Shenanigan'.

```
S h
a n
enanigan
Shenan
Shenan
Shenan
Shenan
Shenanigan
Seaia
Snin
Saa
ShenaniganType
ShenanWabbite
```

Program

```python
# Extract string subparts
s = 'Shenanigan'
print(s[0], s[1])
print(s[4], s[5])
print(s[2:])
print(s[:6])
print(s[:-4])
print(s[-10:-4])
print(s[0:6])
print(s[:])
print(s[0:10:2])
print(s[0:10:3])
print(s[0:10:4])
s = 'Shenanigan'
g = 'Type'
a = s + g
print(a)
s = 'Shenanigan'
t = 'Wabbite'
b = s[:6] + t
print(b)
```

Output

```
S h
a n
enanigan
Shenan
Shenan
Shenan
Shenan
Shenanigan
Seaia
Snin
Saa
ShenaniganType
ShenanWabbite
```

(b) Write a program to convert the following string

'an inferior lawyer with dubious practices'

into

'An Inferior Lawyer With Dubious Practices'

Program

```python
# Capitalize each word of a string
s = 'an inferior lawyer with dubious practices'
t = ''
for w in s.split( ) :
    t = t + w.capitalize( ) + ' '
print(t)
```

Output

```
An Inferior Lawyer With Dubious Practices
```

(c) Write a program to convert the following string
'Light travels faster than sound. This is why some people appear bright until you hear them speak.'

into

'LIGHT travels faster than SOUND. This is why some people appear bright until you hear them speak.'

Program

```
# Search and replace in a string
msg = 'Light travels faster than sound. This is why some people
appear bright until you hear them speak.'
newmsg = msg.replace('Light', 'LIGHT').replace('sound', 'SOUND')
print(newmsg)
```

Output

LIGHT travels faster than SOUND. This is why some people appear bright until you hear them speak.

(d)   What will be the output of the following program?

```
s = 'HumptyDumpty'
print('s = ', s)
print(s.isalpha( ))
print(s.isdigit( ))
print(s.isalnum( ))
print(s.islower( ))
print(s.isupper( ))
print(s.startswith('Hump'))
print(s.endswith('Dump'))
```

Output

```
s =  HumptyDumpty
True
False
True
False
False
True
False
```

(e)   What is the purpose of a raw string?

Answer

Python raw string is created by prefixing a string literal with 'r' or 'R'. Python raw string treats backslash (\) as a literal character. This is useful when we want to have a string that contains backslash and don't want it to be treated as an escape character.

(f)   What is the difference between the functions **ord( )** and **chr( )**?

Answer

ord( ) - Receives a string of length one and returns an integer value representing the Unicode code point of the character.

chr( ) - Receives a Unicode value and returns a string a string of one character corresponding to the Unicode value.

(g)   Each string is an object of which built-in type?

Answer

Each String is an object of **str** built-in type.

(h)   If we wish to work with an individual word in the following string, how will you separate them out:

'The difference between stupidity and genius is that genius has its limits'

Program

```
msg = 'The difference between stupidity and genius is that genius
has its limits'
for word in msg.split( ) :
    print(word)
```

Output

```
The
difference
between
stupidity
and
genius
is
that
genius
has
```

its
limits

[B]   Match the following assuming msg = 'Keep yourself warm'

a. msg.partition(' ')	1. 18
b. msg.split(' ')	2. kEEP YOURSELF WARM
c. msg.startswith('Keep')	3. Keep yourself warm
d. msg.endswith('Keep')	4. 3
e. msg.swapcase( )	5. True
d. msg.capitalize( )	6. False
f. msg.count('e')	7. ['Keep', 'yourself', 'warm']
g. len(msg)	8. ('Keep', ' ', 'yourself warm')

Answer

msg.partition(' ') - ['Keep','','yourself warm']
msg.split(' ') - ['Keep', 'yourself', 'warm']
msg.startswith('Keep') - True
msg.endswith('Keep') - False
msg.swapcase( ) - kEEP YOURSELF WARM
msg.capitalize( ) - Keep yourself warm
msg.count('e') - 3
len(msg) - 18

4 Decision Control Instruction

[A] Answer the following:

(a) Write conditional expressions for

- If a < 10 b = 20, else b = 30
- Print 'Morning' if time < 12, otherwise print 'Afternoon'
- If marks >= 70, set remarks to True, otherwise False

Answer

```
b = 20 if a < 10 else 30
print('Morning')if time < 12 else print('Afternoon')
remarks = 'True' if marks >= 70 else 'False'
```

(b) Rewrite the following code snippet in 1 line:

```
x = 3
y = 3.0
if x == y :
    print('x and y are equal')
else :
    print('x and y are not equal')
```

Answer

```
x, y = 3, 3.0
print('x and y are equal') if x == y else print('x and y are not equal')
```

Output

x and y are equal

[B] What will be the output of the following programs:

(a)
```
i, j, k = 4, -1, 0
w = i or j or k
x = i and j and k
y = i or j and k
z = i and j or k
print(w, x, y, z)
```

Output

4 0 4 -1

(b)
```
a = 10
```

```
a = not not a
print(a)
```

Output

```
True
```

(c)
```
x, y, z = 20,  40,  45
if  x > y and x > z :
    print('biggest = ' + str(x))
elif y > x and y > z :
    print('biggest = ' + str(y))
elif z > x and z > y :
    print('biggest = ' + str(z))
```

Output

```
biggest = 45
```

(d)
```
num = 30
k = 100 if num <= 10 else 500
print(k)
```

Output

```
500
```

(e)
```
a = 10
b = 60
if a and b > 20 :
    print('Hello')
else :
    print('Hi')
```

Output

```
Hello
```

(f)
```
a = 10
b = 60
if a > 20 and b > 20 :
    print('Hello')
else :
    print('Hi')
```

Output

Hi

(g)
```
a = 10
if a = 30 or 40 or 60 :
    print('Hello')
else :
    print('Hi')
```

Output

Error

(h)
```
a = 10
if a = 30 or a == 40 or a == 60 :
    print('Hello')
else :
    print('Hi')
```

Output

Error

(i)
```
a = 10
if a in (30, 40, 50) :
    print('Hello')
else :
    print('Hi')
```

Output

Hi

[C] Point out the errors, if any, in the following programs:

(a)
```
a = 12.25
b = 12.52
if a = b :
    print('a and b are equal')
```

Answer

Error: Invalid syntax. Use a == b

(b)
```
if  ord('X') < ord('x')
    print('Unicode value of X is smaller than that of x')
```

Answer

Error: Invalid syntax. Use : at the end of if as shown below:
if ord('X') < ord('x') :

(c) x = 10
      if x >= 2 then
          print('x')

Answer

Error: Invalid syntax. Use : at the end of if as shown below:
if x >= 2 :

(d) x = 10 ; y = 15
      if x % 2 = y % 3
          print('Carpathians\n')

Answer

Error: Invalid syntax. Use == in place of = during comparison

(e) x, y = 30, 40
      if x == y :
          print('x is equal to y')
      elseif x > y :
          print('x is greater than y')
      elseif x < y :
          print('x is less than y')

Answer

Error: Invalid syntax. Use **elif** in place of **elseif**

[D] If a = 10, b = 12, c = 0, find the values of the following expressions:

      a != 6 and b > 5
      a == 9 or b < 3
      not (a < 10)
      not (a > 5 and c)
      5 and c != 8 or c

Answer

True
False
True

True
True

[E] Attempt the following:

(a) Any integer is input through the keyboard. Write a program to find out whether it is an odd number or even number.

Program

```
# Determine whether number is odd or even
x = int(input('Enter any number: '))
j = 2
if x % j == 0 :
    print('Even Number')
else :
    print('Odd Number')
```

Output

```
Enter any number: 48
Even Number
```

(b) Any year is input through the keyboard. Write a program to determine whether the year is a leap year or not.

Program

```
# Determine whether year is leap or not
year = int(input('Enter a year: '))
if year % 4 == 0 :
    if year % 100 == 0 :
        if year % 400 == 0 :
            print(year, 'is a Leap Year')
        else :
            print(year, 'is not a Leap Year')
    else :
        print(year, 'is a Leap Year')
else :
    print(year, 'is not a Leap Year')
```

Output

```
Enter a year: 1996
1996 is a Leap Year
```

```
Enter a year: 2000
2000 is a Leap Year

Enter a year: 1900
1900 is not a Leap Year
```

(c)　If ages of Ram, Shyam and Ajay are input through the keyboard, write a program to determine the youngest of the three.

Program

```
# Determine youngest out of three persons
ram_age = int(input('Enter Ram\'s age: '))
shyam_age = int(input('Enter Shyam\'s age: '))
ajay_age = int(input('Enter Ajay\'s: '))
if ram_age < shyam_age and ram_age < ajay_age :
    print('Youngest is Ram')
elif shyam_age < ram_age and shyam_age < ajay_age :
    print('Youngest is Shyam')
elif ajay_age < ram_age and ajay_age < shyam_age :
    print('Youngest is Ajay')
```

Output

```
Enter Ram's age: 23
Enter Shyam's age: 45
Enter Ajay's: 34
Youngest is Ram
```

(d)　Write a program to check whether a triangle is valid or not, when the three angles of the triangle are entered through the keyboard. A triangle is valid if the sum of all the three angles is equal to 180 degrees.

Program

```
# Determine whether triangle is valid or not
x = int(input('Enter angle no. 1: '))
y = int(input('Enter angle no. 2: '))
z = int(input('Enter angle no. 3: '))
sum_of_angles = x + y + z
if sum_of_angles == 180 :
    print('Valid Triangle')
```

```
else :
    print('Is not a Valid Triangle')
```

Output

```
Enter angle no. 1: 45
Enter angle no. 2: 45
Enter angle no. 3: 90
Valid Triangle
```

(e) Write a program to find the absolute value of a number entered through the keyboard.

Program

```
# Obtain absolute value of a number
x = int(input('Enter any number: '))
if x < 0 :
    y = x * (-1)
else :
    y = x
print('Absolute value of', x, 'is', y)
```

Output

```
Enter any number: -20
Absolute value of -20 is 20

Enter any number: 23
Absolute value of 23 is 23
```

(f) Given the length and breadth of a rectangle, write a program to find whether the area of the rectangle is greater than its perimeter. For example, the area of the rectangle with length = 5 and breadth = 4 is greater than its perimeter.

Program

```
# Determine whether area of rectangle is greater than its perimeter
length = int(input('Enter length of rectangle: '))
breadth = int(input('Enter breadth of rectangle: '))

area = length * breadth
perimeter = 2 * (length + breadth)
```

```
print('Area =', area, 'Perimeter =', perimeter)
if area > perimeter :
    print('Area of Rectangle is greater than perimeter')
else :
    print('Perimeter of Rectangle is greater than area')
```

Output

```
Enter length of rectangle: 4
Enter breadth of rectangle: 5
Area = 20 Perimeter = 18
Area of Rectangle is greater than perimeter

Enter length of rectangle: 2
Enter breadth of rectangle: 1
Area = 2 Perimeter = 6
Perimeter of Rectangle is greater than area
```

(g) Given three points **(x1, y1)**, **(x2, y2)** and **(x3, y3)**, write a program to check if all the three points fall on one straight line.

Program

```
# Determine whether 3 points are collinear
x1 = int(input('Enter the co-ordinate of x1: '))
y1 = int(input('Enter the co-ordinate of y1: '))
x2 = int(input('Enter the co-ordinate of x2: '))
y2 = int(input('Enter the co-ordinate of y2: '))
x3 = int(input('Enter the co-ordinate of x3: '))
y3 = int(input('Enter the co-ordinate of y3: '))

if x1 == x2 and x2 == x3 :
    print('Collinear')
elif x1 != x2 and x2 != x3 and x3 != x1 :
    # Calculate Slope of line between each pair of points
    s1 = (float(abs(y2 - y1))) / (float(abs(x2 - x1)))
    s2 = (float(abs(y3 - y2))) / (float(abs(x3 - x2)))
    s3 = (float(abs(y3 - y1))) / (float(abs(x3 - x1)))

    if s1 == s2 and s2 == s3 :
        print('Collinear')
    else :
        print('Non Collinear')
```

```
else :
   print('Non Collinear')
```

Output

```
Enter the co-ordinate of x1: 4
Enter the co-ordinate of y1: 4
Enter the co-ordinate of x2: 5
Enter the co-ordinate of y2: 5
Enter the co-ordinate of x3: 6
Enter the co-ordinate of y3: 6
All the 3 points lies on the one straight line
```

(h) Given the coordinates **(x, y)** of center of a circle and its radius, write a program that will determine whether a point lies inside the circle, on the circle or outside the circle. (Hint: Use **sqrt( )** and **pow( )** functions)

Program

```
# Determine whether point lies inside, outside or on the circle
import math

centerX = int(input('Enter X coord. of center of circle: ' ))
centerY = int(input('Enter Y coord. of center of circle: ' ))

radius = int(input('Enter radius of circle: '))

print('Enter coordinates of point:')
pointX = int(input('Enter X coord. of point: '))
pointY = int(input('Enter Y coord. of point: '))

xDiff = centerX - pointX ;
yDiff = centerY - pointY ;

distance = math.sqrt((xDiff * xDiff) + (yDiff * yDiff))

if distance == radius :
   print('Point is on the circle')
elif distance < radius :
   print('Point lies inside the circle')
else :
```

```
        print('Point lies outside the circle')
```

Output

```
Enter X coord. of center of circle: 0
Enter Y coord. of center of circle: 0
Enter radius of circle: 5
Enter coordinates of point:
Enter X coord. of point: 5
Enter Y coord. of point: 0
Point is on the circle
```

(i) Given a point **(x, y)**, write a program to find out if it lies on the X-axis, Y-axis or on the origin.

Program

```
# Determine where a point lies in coordinate system
x = int(input('Enter X Coord of the point:'))
y = int(input('Enter Y coord of the point:'))

if x == 0 and y == 0 :
    print('Point is the origin')
elif x == 0 and y != 0 :
    print('Point lies on the Y axis')
elif x != 0 and y == 0 :
    print('Point lies on the X axis')
else :
    if x > 0 and y > 0 :
        print('Point lies in the First Quadrant')
    elif x < 0 and y > 0 :
        print('Point lies in the Second Quadrant')
    elif x < 0 and y < 0 :
        print('Point lies in the Third Quadrant')
    else :
        print('Point lies in the Fourth Quadrant')
```

Output

```
Enter X Coord of the point:0
Enter Y coord of the point:0
Point is the origin
```

```
Enter X Coord of the point:-10
Enter Y coord of the point:-20
Point lies in the Third Quadrant
```

(j) A year is entered through the keyboard, write a program to determine whether the year is leap or not. Use the logical operators **and** and **or**.

Program

```python
# Determine whether year is leap or not
year = int(input('Enter a year: '))
if (year % 4 == 0 and year % 100 != 0) or year % 400 == 0 :
    print(year, 'is a leap year')
else :
    print(year, 'is not a leap year')
```

Output

```
Enter a year: 2016
2016 is a Leap Year
```

(k) If the three sides of a triangle are entered through the keyboard, write a program to check whether the triangle is valid or not. The triangle is valid if the sum of two sides is greater than the largest of the three sides.

Program

```python
# Determine whether triangle is valid or not
s1 = int(input('Enter the 1st side of triangle: '))
s2 = int(input('Enter the 2nd side of triangle: '))
s3 = int(input('Enter the 3rd side of triangle: '))
if s1 + s2 <= s3 or s2 + s3 <= s1 or s1 + s3 <= s2 :
    print('Invalid Triangle')
else :
    print('Valid Triangle')
```

Output

```
Enter the 1st side of triangle: 6
Enter the 2nd side of triangle: 7
Enter the 3rd side of triangle: 10
Valid Triangle
```

```
Enter the 1st side of triangle: 5
Enter the 2nd side of triangle: 3
Enter the 3rd side of triangle: 12
```

(l)　If the three sides of a triangle are entered through the keyboard, write a program to check whether the triangle is isosceles, equilateral, scalene or right angled triangle.

Program

```python
# Determine the type of triangle
s1 = int(input('Enter the 1st side of triangle: '))
s2 = int(input('Enter the 2nd side of triangle: '))
s3 = int(input('Enter the 3rd side of triangle: '))

if s1 + s2 <= s3 or s2 + s3 <= s1 or s1 + s3 <= s2 :
    print('The sides do not form a triangle')
else :
    if s1 != s2 and s2 != s3 and s3 != s1 :
        print('Scalene triangle')

    if s1 == s2 and s2 != s3 :
        print('Isosceles triangle')

    if s2 == s3 and s3 != s1 :
        print('Isosceles triangle')

    if s1 == s3 and s3 != s2 :
        print('Isosceles triangle')

    if s1 == s2 and s2 == s3 :
        print('Equilateral triangle')

    a = ( s1 * s1) == ( s2 * s2) + ( s3 * s3)
    b = ( s2 * s2) == ( s1 * s1) + ( s3 * s3)
    c = ( s3 * s3) == ( s1 * s1) + ( s2 * s2)

    if a or b or c :
        print('Right-angled triangle')
```

Output

```
Enter the 1st side of triangle: 6
Enter the 2nd side of triangle: 8
Enter the 3rd side of triangle: 10
Scalene triangle
Right-angled triangle

Enter the 1st side of triangle: 3
Enter the 2nd side of triangle: 3
Enter the 3rd side of triangle: 3
Equilateral triangle

Enter the 1st side of triangle: 5
Enter the 2nd side of triangle: 3
Enter the 3rd side of triangle: 12
The sides do not form a triangle
```

5 Repetition Control Instruction

[A] Answer the following:

(a) When does the **else** block of a **while** loop go to work?

Answer

Else block is optional. If present, it is executed when condition fails.

(b) What happens when a **pass** statement is executed?

Answer

The pass statement is a null operation; nothing happens when it executes.

(c) Can **range( )** function be used to generate numbers from 0.1 to 1.0 in steps of 0.1?

Answer

No. **range( )** function cannot generate float numbers.

(d) Can a **while** loop be nested within a **for** loop and vice versa?

Answer

Yes a **while** loop can be nested within a **for** loop and vice versa.

(e) Can a **while/for** loop be used in an **if/else** and vice versa?

Answer

Yes a **while/for** loop be used in an **if/else** and vice versa.

[B] Match the following for the values each **range( )** function will generated when used in a **for** loop.

a. range(5)	1. 1, 2, 3, 4
b. range(1, 10, 3)	2. 0, 1, 2, 3, 4
c. range(10, 1, -2)	3. Nothing
d. range(1, 5)	4. 10, 8, 6, 4, 2
e. range(-2)	5. 1, 4, 7

Answer

range(5) - 0, 1, 2, 3, 4
range(1, 10, 3) - 1, 4, 7

```
range(10, 1, -2) - 10, 8, 6, 4, 2
range(1, 5) - 1, 2, 3, 4, 5
range(-2) - Nothing
```

[C] Attempt the following:

(a) Write a program to print first 25 odd numbers using **range( )**.

Program

```python
# Generate first 25 odd numbers
j = 1
print('First 25 Odd Numbers:')
for i in range(50) :
    if i % j == 1 :
        print(i, end = ', ')
    i += 1
```

Output

```
First 25 Odd Numbers:
1, 3, 5, 7, 9, 11, 13, 15, 17, 19, 21, 23, 25, 27, 29, 31, 33, 35, 37, 39,
41, 43, 45, 47, 49,
```

(b) Rewrite the following program using for loop.

```python
lst = ['desert', 'dessert', 'to', 'too', 'lose', 'loose']
s = 'Mumbai'
i = 0
while i < len(lst) :
    if i > 3 :
        break
    else :
        print(i, lst[i], s[i])
        i += 1
```

Program

```python
# Rewrite using for loop
lst = ['desert','dessert','to','too','lose','loose']
s = 'Mumbai'
i = 0
for i, ele in enumerate(lst) :
    if i > 3 :
```

```
    break
print(i, ele, s[i])
```

Output

```
0 desert M
1 dessert u
2 to m
3 too b
```

(c) Write a program to count the number of alphabets and number of digits in the string 'Nagpur-440010'.

Program

```
# Count alphabets, digits and special symbols in a string
string = 'Nagpur-440010'
alphabets = digits = special = 0

for i in range(len(string)) :
    if(string[i].isalpha( )) :
        alphabets = alphabets + 1
    elif(string[i].isdigit( )) :
        digits = digits + 1
    else :
        special = special + 1

print('Number of Alphabets =', alphabets)
print('Number of Digits =', digits)
print('Number of Special Characters =', special)
```

Output

```
Number of Alphabets = 6
Number of Digits = 6
Number of Special Characters = 1
```

(d) A five-digit number is entered through the keyboard. Write a program to obtain the reversed number and to determine whether the original and reversed numbers are equal or not.

Program

```python
# Reverse a 5-digit number and compare with original
num = int(input('Enter a 5-digit number: '))
orinum = num
revnum = 0
while(num > 0) :
    rem = num % 10
    revnum = (revnum * 10) + rem
    num = num // 10

print('Original number =', orinum)
print('Reversed number = ', revnum)
if orinum == revnum :
    print('Original and reversed numbers are same')
else :
    print('Original and reversed numbers are different')
```

Output

```
Enter a 5-digit number: 12345
Original number = 12345
Reversed number =  54321
Original and reversed number are different

Enter a 5-digit number: 12221
Original number = 12221
Reversed number =  12221
Original and reversed numbers are same
```

(e) Write a program to find the factorial value of any number entered through the keyboard.

Program

```python
number = int(input('Enter a number: '))
fact = 1
for i in range(1, number + 1) :
    fact = fact * i
print('Factorial value = ', fact)
```

Output

```
Enter a number: 5
Factorial value =  120
```

(f)   Write a program to print out all Armstrong numbers between 1 and 500. If sum of cubes of each digit of the number is equal to the number itself, then the number is called an Armstrong number. For example, 153 = (1 * 1 * 1) + (5 * 5 * 5) + (3 * 3 * 3).

Program

```python
print('Armstrong numbers between 1 and 500 are:')
for num in range(1, 501) :
    n = num
    d3 = n % 10
    n = int(n / 10)
    d2 = n % 10
    n = int(n / 10)
    d1 = n % 10
    if d1 * d1 * d1 + d2 * d2 * d2 + d3 * d3 * d3 == num :
        print(num)
```

Output

```
Armstrong numbers between 1 and 500 are:
1
153
370
371
407
```

(g)   Write a program to print all prime numbers from 1 to 300.

Program

```python
lower = 1
upper = 300
print('All Prime numbers from 1 to 300:')
for num in range(lower, upper + 1) :
    for n in range(2, num) :
        if (num % n) == 0 :
            break
```

```
    else :
        print(num, end = ', ')
```

Output

All Prime numbers from 1 to 300:
1, 2, 3, 5, 7, 11, 13, 17, 19, 23, 29, 31, 37, 41, 43, 47, 53, 59, 61, 67, 71, 73, 79, 83, 89, 97, 101, 103, 107, 109, 113, 127, 131, 137, 139, 149, 151, 157, 163, 167, 173, 179, 181, 191, 193, 197, 199, 211, 223, 227, 229, 233, 239, 241, 251, 257, 263, 269, 271, 277, 281, 283, 293,

(h) Write a program to print the multiplication table of the number entered by the user. The table should get displayed in the following form:

```
29 * 1 = 29
29 * 2 = 58

...
```

Program

```
num = int(input('Enter any number: '))
lower = 1
upper = 10
for i in range(lower, upper + 1) :
    print(num, 'x', i , '=' , num * i)
```

Output

```
Enter any number: 29
29 x 1 = 29
29 x 2 = 58
29 x 3 = 87
29 x 4 = 116
29 x 5 = 145
29 x 6 = 174
29 x 7 = 203
29 x 8 = 232
29 x 9 = 261
29 x 10 = 290
```

(i) When interest compounds **q** times per year at an annual rate of **r** % for **n** years, the principal **p** compounds to an amount **a** as per the following formula:

$$a = p\left(1 + r / q\right)^{nq}$$

Write a program to read 10 sets of **p, r, n** & **q** and calculate the corresponding **a**s.

Program

```
for i in range(10) :
    p = float(input('Enter value of p: '))
    r = float(input('Enter value of r: '))
    n = float(input('Enter value of n: '))
    q = float(input('Enter value of q: '))
    a = p * ((1 + r / 100 / q) ** (n * q))
    print('Compound Interest = Rs.', a)
```

Output

```
Enter value of p: 1000
Enter value of r: 5
Enter value of n: 3
Enter value of q: 4
Compound Interest = Rs. 1160.7545177229981
...
```

(j) Write a program to generate all Pythagorean Triplets with side length less than or equal to 30.

Program

```
n = 31
for i in range(1, n) :
    for j in range((i + 1), (n + 1), 1) :
        t = (i * i) + (j * j)
        for k in range((i + 2), (n + 1), 1) :
            if (t == k * k) :
                print(i , j, k)
```

Output

```
3 4 5
5 12 13
6 8 10
7 24 25
8 15 17
9 12 15
10 24 26
12 16 20
15 20 25
18 24 30
20 21 29
```

(k) Population of a town today is 100000. The population has increased steadily at the rate of 10 % per year for last 10 years. Write a program to determine the population at the end of each year in the last decade.

Program

```python
population = 100000
for i in range(10) :
    population += int(population * 10 / 100)
    print('Year', i + 1, ':', population)
```

Output

```
Year 1 : 110000
Year 2 : 121000
Year 3 : 133100
Year 4 : 146410
Year 5 : 161051
Year 6 : 177156
Year 7 : 194871
Year 8 : 214358
Year 9 : 235793
Year 10 : 259372
```

(l) Ramanujan number is the smallest number that can be expressed as sum of two cubes in two different ways. Write a program to print all such numbers up to a reasonable limit.

Program

```python
print('Ramanujan Numbers:')
for i in range(1, 31):
  for j in range(1, 31):
    for k in range(1, 31):
      for l in range(1, 31):
        if (i != j and i != k and i != l) and (j != k and j != l)
                and (k != l) :
          if i * i * i + j * j * j == k * k * k + l * l * l :
            print(i, j, k, l)
```

Output

```
Ramanujan Numbers:
1    12   9    10
1    12   10   9
2    16   9    15
2    16   15   9

.. .. .. .. .. ..
```

(m) Write a program to print 24 hours of day with suitable suffixes like
     AM, PM, Noon and Midnight.

Program

```python
for hour in range(24) :
  if hour == 0 :
    print('12 Midnight')
    continue
  if hour < 12 :
    print(hour, 'AM')
  if hour == 12 :
    print('12 Noon')
  if hour > 12 :
    print(hour % 12, 'PM')
```

Output

```
12 Midnight
1 AM
2 AM
.. ..
```

6 Console Input Output

[A] Attempt the following:

(a) How will you make the following code more compact?

```
print('Enter ages of 3 persons')
age1 = input( )
age2 = input( )
age3 = input( )
```

Answer

```
age1, age2, age3 = input('Enter 3 values: ').split(',')
```

Output

```
Enter 3 values: 45, 44, 47
```

(b) Write a program to receive an arbitrary number of floats using one **input( )** statement. Calculate the average of floats received.

Program

```
# Receive arbitrary number of floats
num = int(input('How many numbers do you wish to input: '))
totalsum = 0
number = [float(x) for x in input('Enter all numbers: ').split( )]
for n in range(len(number)) :
    totalsum = totalsum + number[n]
avg = totalsum / num
print('Average of', num, 'numbers is:', avg)
```

Output

```
How many numbers do you wish to input: 5
Enter all numbers: 10 20 30 40 50
Average of 5 numbers is: 30.0
```

(c) Write a program to receive the following using one **input( )** statement.

```
Name of the person
Years of service
Diwali bonus received
```

Calculate and print the agreement deduction as per the following formula:

deduction = 2 * years of service + bonus * 5.5 / 100

Program

```
data = input('Name, year of service, diwali bonus: ').split(',')
name = data[0]
yos = int(data[1])
bonus = float(data[2])
deduction = float((2 * yos + bonus * 5.5 ) / 100)
print('Deduction = Rs.', deduction)
```

Output

```
Name, year of service, diwali bonus: Ramesh, 3, 9500
Deduction = Rs. 522.56
```

(d)　Write a program to print the values

a = 12.34, b = 234.39, c = 444.34, d = 1.23, e = 34.67

as shown below:

```
a =     12.34
b =    234.39
c =    444.34
d =      1.23
e =     34.67
```

Program

```
a, b, c, d, e = 12.34, 234.39, 444.34, 1.23, 34.67
print(f'a = {a:>10}')
print(f'b = {b:>10}')
print(f'c = {c:>10}')
print(f'd = {d:>10}')
print(f'e = {e:>10}')
```

Output

```
a =     12.34
b =    234.39
c =    444.34
```

```
d =      1.23
e =      34.67
```

[B] Match the following:

```
a. Default value of sep in print( )   1. ' '
b. Default value of end in print( )   2. Using fstring
c. Easiest way to print output        3. Right justify num in 5 columns
d. Return type of split( )            4. Left justify num in 5 columns
e. print('{num:>5}')                  5. str
d. print('{num:<5}')                  6. \n
```

Answer

```
Default value of sep in print( ) - ' '
Default value of end in print( ) - \n
Easiest way to print output - Using fstring
Return type of split( ) - str
print('{num:>5}') - Right justify num in 5 columns
print('{num:<5}') - Left justify num in 5 columns
```

7 Lists

[A] Answer the following:

(a) Write a program to create a list of 5 odd integers. Replace the third element with a list of 4 even integers. Flatten, sort and print the list.

Program

```
# Modify, flatten and sort list
x = [1, 3, 5, 7, 9]
y = [2, 4, 6, 8]
x[2] = y
print(x)
x = x[:2] + [*y] + x[3:]
print(x)
x.sort( )
print(x)
```

Output

```
[1, 3, [2, 4, 6, 8], 7, 9]
[1, 3, 2, 4, 6, 8, 7, 9]
[1, 2, 3, 4, 6, 7, 8, 9]
```

(b) Suppose a list contains 20 integers generated randomly. Receive a number from the keyboard and report position of all occurrences of this number in the list.

Program

```
# Report number of occurrences of a number in the list
import random
lst = [ ]
for k in range(20) :
    n = random.randint(0, 50)
    lst.append(n)
print(lst)

num = int(input('Enter number: '))
count = 0
for i in range(len(lst)) :
    if lst[i] == num:
        print('Number found at position:', i)
```

Output

```
[44, 4, 22, 11, 36, 29, 38, 32, 14, 34, 48, 49, 4, 14, 23, 5, 28, 43, 49,
3]
Enter number: 14
Number found at position: 8
Number found at position: 13
```

(c) Suppose a list has 20 numbers. Write a program that removes all duplicates from this list.

Program

```
# Remove duplicates in a list
lst = [1, 2, 3, 4, 5, 1, 2, 3, 4, 5, 10, 20, 68, 8, 40, 45, 1, 5, 53, 45, 17]
print('Original list: ', lst)
final_lst=[ ]
for num in lst :
    if num not in final_lst :
        final_lst.append(num)

lst = final_lst
print('List after removing duplicates:', lst)
```

Output

```
Original list:  [1, 2, 3, 4, 5, 1, 2, 3, 4, 5, 10, 20, 68, 8, 40, 45, 1, 5, 53,
45, 17]
List after removing duplicates: [1, 2, 3, 4, 5, 10, 20, 68, 8, 40, 45, 53,
17]
```

(d) Suppose a list contains positive and negative numbers. Write a program to create two lists—one containing positive numbers and another containing negative numbers.

Program

```
# Separate positive and negative numbers into two lists
lst1 = [1, -9, -6, -45, -78,-1, 2, 3, 4, 5]
lst2 = [ ]
lst3 = [ ]
count, ncount = 0, 0
for num in lst1 :
```

```
   if num >= 0 :
      lst2.append(num)
   else :
      lst3.append(num)

print('Original list:', lst1)
print('Positive numbers list:', lst2)
print('Negative numbers list:', lst3)
```

Output

```
Original list: [1, -9, -6, -45, -78, -1, 2, 3, 4, 5]
Positive numbers list: [1, 2, 3, 4, 5]
Negative numbers list: [-9, -6, -45, -78, -1]
```

(e) Suppose a list contains 5 strings. Write a program to convert all these strings to uppercase.

Program

```
# Converts strings in a list to uppercase
lst = ['abc', 'def', 'ghi', 'jkl', 'lmn']
for i, item in enumerate(lst) :
   lst[i] = item.upper( )

print(lst)
```

Output

```
['ABC', 'DEF', 'GHI', 'JKL', 'LMN']
```

(f) Write a program that converts list of temperatures in Fahrenheit degrees to equivalent Celsius degrees.

Program

```
# Conver farhrenheit temperatures in list into centigrade
fahr = [212, 120, 100, 93, 37]
for i, f in enumerate(fahr) :
   c = int(5 / 9 * (f - 32))
   fahr[i] = c
   print(f, c)
print(fahr)
```

Output

```
212 100
120 48
100 37
93 33
37 2
[100, 48, 37, 33, 2]
```

(g) Write a program to obtain a median value of a list of numbers, without disturbing the order of the numbers in the list.

Program

```
# Obtain median of a list
num = [1, 2, 3, 4, 5, 6, 7]
n = len(num)
if n % 2 == 0 :
    i = int(n / 2 - 1)
    j = int(n / 2)
    median = (num[i] + num[j]) / 2
else :
    i = int(n / 2)
    median = num[i]

print('Median value =', median)
```

Output

```
Median value = 4
```

(h) A list contains only positive and negative integers. Write a program to obtain the number of negative numbers present in the list, without using a loop.

Program

```
# Count negatives in a list without using a loop
lst = [1, 2, 3, 4, 5, -1, -2, -3, -4, -5]
if 0 not in lst :
    lst.append(0)
lst = sorted(lst)
pos = lst.index(0)
```

```
print('Number of negative numbers in the list =', pos)
```

Output

Number of negative numbers in the list = 5

8

Tuples

[A] Answer the following:

(a) Suppose a date is represented as a tuple (d, m, y). Write a program to create two date tuples and find the number of days between the two dates.

Program

```
# Determine number of days between two dates
dt1 = (17, 3, 1998)
dt2 = (17, 4, 2011)

d1, m1, y1 = dt1[0], dt1[1], dt1[2]
d2, m2, y2 = dt2[0], dt2[1], dt2[2]
days1 = [31, 0, 31, 30, 31, 30, 31, 31, 30, 31, 30, 31]
days2 = [31, 0, 31, 30, 31, 30, 31, 31, 30, 31, 30, 31]

ndays1 = (y1 - 1) * 365
ldays1 = ((y1 - 1) // 4) - ((y1 - 1) // 100) + ((y1 - 1) // 400)
tdays1 = ndays1 + ldays1

if((y1 % 4 == 0 and y1 % 100 != 0) or (y1 % 400 == 0)) :
    days1[1] = 29
else :
    days1[1] = 28

s1 = sum(days1[0:m1 - 1])
tdays1 += s1

ndays2 = (y2 - 1) * 365
ldays2 = ((y2 -1) // 4) - ((y2 - 1) // 100) + ((y2 - 1) // 400)
tdays2 = ndays2 + ldays2

if((y2 % 4 == 0 and y2 % 100 != 0) or (y2 % 400 == 0)) :
    days2[1] = 29
else :
    days2[1] = 28

s2 = sum(days2[0:m2 - 1])
tdays2 += s2

diff = tdays2 - tdays1
```

```
print('Difference in days = ', diff)
```

Output

```
Difference in days =  4779
```

(b) Create a list of tuples. Each tuple should contain an item and its price in float. Write a program to sort the tuples in descending order by price. Hint: Use **operator.itemgetter( )**.

Program

```
import operator
lst = [('Key', 101.25), ('Lock', 320.85), ('Hammer', 100.55),
('Spanner', 67.77), ('Tong', 93.03)]
print(sorted(lst, reverse = True, key = operator.itemgetter(1)))
```

Output

```
[('Lock', 320.85), ('Key', 101.25), ('Hammer', 100.55), ('Tong', 93.03),
('Spanner', 67.77)]
```

(c) Store the data about shares held by a user as tuples containing the following information about shares:

```
Share name
Date of purchase
Cost price
Number of shares
Selling price
```

Write a program to determine:

- Total cost of the portfolio.
- Total amount gained or lost.
- Percentage profit made or loss incurred.

Program

```
lst = [ ]
i = 0

num_companies = int(input('Enter no. of companies: '))
for i in range(num_companies):
```

```python
name = input('Enter name: ')
no_of_shares = int(input('Enter no of shares: '))
dt_of_pur = input('Enter date of purchase: ')
cost_price = int(input('Enter Cost price: '))
selling_price = int(input('Enter selling price: '))
tpl = (name, no_of_shares, dt_of_pur, cost_price, selling_price)
lst.append(tpl)


tot = 0
gaintot = 0
losstot = 0
for l in lst :
  no_of_shares = l[1]
  cost_price = l[3]
  selling_price = l[4]
  cop = int(no_of_shares * cost_price)
  tot = tot + cop

  if selling_price > cost_price :
    gaintot += (selling_price - cost_price) * no_of_shares
  else :
    losstot += (cost_price - selling_price) * no_of_shares

print(f'Total cost of portfolio:{tot:.2f}')

if gaintot > losstot :
  net = gaintot - losstot
  gain_per = net / tot * 100
  print(f'Net amount gained:{net:.2f}')
  print(f'Percentage profit:{gain_per:.2f}')
else :
  net = losstot - gaintot
  loss_per = net / tot * 100
  print(f'Net amount lost:{net:.2f}')
  print(f'Percentage loss:{loss_per:.2f}')
```

Output

```
Enter no. of companies: 3
Enter name: L and T
Enter no of shares: 100
Enter date of purchase: 12/12/2012
```

```
Enter Cost price: 145
Enter selling price: 186
Enter name: Tata Motors
Enter no of shares: 120
Enter date of purchase: 13/11/2016
Enter Cost price: 785
Enter selling price: 678
Enter name: Infosys
Enter no of shares: 90
Enter date of purchase: 14/05/2018
Enter Cost price: 775
Enter selling price: 800
Total cost of portfolio: 178450.00
Net amount lost: 6490.00
Percentage loss: 3.64
```

(d) Write a program to remove empty tuple from a list of tuples.

Program

```
lst1= [( ), ('Paras', 5), ('Ankit', 11), ( ), ('Harsha', 115), ('Aditya', 115),
( ), ('Aditi', 3), ( )]
lst2 = [ ]
for item in lst1 :
    if len(item) != 0 :
        lst2.append(item)
print(lst2)
```

Output

```
[('Paras', 5), ('Ankit', 11), ('Harsha', 115), ('Aditya', 115), ('Aditi', 3)]
```

(e) Write a program to create following 3 lists:
     - a list of names
     - a list of roll numbers
     - a list of marks

Generate and print a list of tuples containing name, roll number and marks from the 3 lists. From this list generate 3 tuples—one containing all names, another containing all roll numbers and third containing all marks.

Program

```
name = ['Aditi' , 'Mrunal' , 'Aditya' , 'Girish' , 'Ankit' , 'Meenal']
rollno = ['12' , '43' , '45' , '50' , '66' , '21']
marks = ['90' , '45' , '82' , '75' , '95' , '65']
t1 = tuple(name)
t2 = tuple(rollno)
t3 = tuple(marks)
lst = [t1, t2, t3]
print(lst)
print(t1)
print(t2)
print(t3)
```

Output

```
[('Aditi', 'Mrunal', 'Aditya', 'Girish', 'Ankit', 'Meenal'), ('12', '43', '45',
'50', '66', '21'), ('90', '45', '82', '75', '95', '65')]
('Aditi', 'Mrunal', 'Aditya', 'Girish', 'Ankit', 'Meenal')
('12', '43', '45', '50', '66', '21')
('90', '45', '82', '75', '95', '65')
```

[B] Match the following for the values each **range( )** function will generated when used in a **for** loop.

a. tpl1 = ('A',)	1. tuple of length 6
b. tpl1 = ('A')	2. tuple of lists
c. t = tpl[::-1]	3. Tuple
d. ('A', 'B', 'C', 'D')	4. list of tuples
e. [(1, 2), (2, 3), (4, 5)]	5. String
f. tpl = tuple(range(2, 5))	6. Sorts tuple
g. ([1, 2], [3, 4], [5, 6])	7. (2, 3, 4)
h. t = tuple('Ajooba')	8. tuple of strings
i. [*a, *b, *c]	9. Unpacking of tuples in a list
j. (*a, *b, *c)	10. Unpacking of lists in a tuple

Answer

```
tpl1 = ('A',) - Tuple
tpl1 = ('A') - String
t = tpl[::-1] - Sorts tuple
('A' , 'B' , 'C' , 'D') - tuple of strings
[(1, 2), (2, 3), (4, 5)] - list of tuples
```

```
tpl = tuple(range(2, 5)) - (2, 3, 4)
([1, 2], [3, 4], [5, 6]) - tuple of lists
t = tuple('Ajooba') - tuple of length 6
[*a , *b, *c] - Unpacking of tuples in a list
(*a , *b, *c) - Unpacking of lists in a tuple
```

[C] Which of the following properties apply to string, list and tuple?

- Iterable
- Sliceable
- Indexable
- Immutable
- Sequence
- Can be empty
- Sorted collection
- Ordered collection
- Unordered collection
- Elements can be accessed using their position in the collection

Answer

Iterable - string, list and tuple
Sliceable - string, list and tuple
Indexable - string, list and tuple
Immutable - string, tuple
Sequence - string, list and tuple
Can be empty - string, list and tuple
Sorted collection - none
Ordered collection - string, list and tuple
Unordered collection - string
Elements can be accessed using their position in the collection - string, list and tuple

[D] Which of the following operations can be performed on string, list and tuple?

- a = b + c
- a += b
- Appending a new element at the end
- Deletion of an element at the 0th position
- Modification of last element
- In place reversal

Answer

a = b + c - string, list and tuple
a += b - string, list and tuple
Appending a new element at the end - list
Deletion of an element at the 0th position - list
Modification of last element - string, list and tuple
In place reversal - list

9 Sets

[A] Answer the following:

(a) A set contains names which begin either with A or with B. write a program to separate out the names into two sets, one containing names beginning with A and another containing names beginning with B.

Program

```
# Split given set into two sets
lst = {'Aditya', 'Aditi', 'Ankita', 'Aniket', 'Anuja', 'Bhushan', 'Bahu',
'Bali', 'Bhoomi', 'Babhoti' }
t = set( )
s = set( )
for item in lst :
    if item.startswith('A') :
        t.add(item)
    elif item.startswith('B') :
        s.add(item)
print(s)
print(t)
```

Output

```
{'Bhoomi', 'Bahu', 'Babhoti', 'Bali', 'Bhushan'}
{'Anuja', 'Ankita', 'Aditya', 'Aniket', 'Aditi'}
```

(b) Create an empty set. Write a program that adds five new names to this set, modifies one existing name and deletes two names existing in it.

Program

```
# Set operations
s = set( )
s.add('Amol')
s.add('Priya')
s.add('Mira')
s.add('Dipti')
s.add('Anil')
print('After adding 5 names:', s)
s.remove('Anil')
s.add('ANIL')
```

```
print('After modifying Anil:', s)
s.remove('Dipti')
s.remove('Mira')
print('After deleting Dipti and Mira:', s)
```

Output

```
After adding 5 names: {'Priya', 'Dipti', 'Anil', 'Mira', 'Amol'}
After modifying Anil: {'Priya', 'ANIL', 'Dipti', 'Mira', 'Amol'}
After deleting Dipti and Mira: {'Priya', 'ANIL', 'Amol'}
```

(c) What is the difference between the two set functions—**discard( )** and **remove( )**.

Answer

remove( ) raises an exception when the element which we are trying to remove is not present in the set, whereas, **discard( )** doesn't.

(d) Write a program to create a set containing 10 randomly generated numbers in the range 15 to 45. Count how many of these numbers are less than 30. Delete all numbers which are greater than 35.

Program

```
# Set operations
import random
s = set( )
while True :
    s.add(random.randint(15, 45))
    if len(s) == 10 :
        break
print('Oringal set:', s)
t = set( )
count = 0
for item in s :
    if item < 30 :
        count += 1
    if item <= 35 :
        t.add(item)

s = t
```

```
print('Count of nos. less than 30:', count)
print('Set after deleting elements > 35: ', s)
```

Output

```
Oringal set: {32, 34, 40, 15, 16, 22, 23, 24, 25, 27}
Count of nos. less than 30: 7
Set after deleting elements > 35:  {32, 34, 15, 16, 22, 23, 24, 25, 27}
```

(e) What do the following set operators do?

|, &, ^, -

Answer

```
|   Union of two sets
&   Intersection of two sets
^   Symmetric difference between two sets
-   Difference between two sets
```

(f) What do the following set operators do?

|=, &=, ^=, -=

Answer

|= performs union of two sets and stores the result in left operand.

&= performs intersection of two sets and stores result in left operand.

^= Finds symmetric difference between two sets and stores result in left operand.

-= Finds difference between two sets and stores result in left operand.

(g) How will you remove all duplicate elements present in a string, a list and a tuple?

Answer

```
# Delete duplicates from string, list and tuple
s = 'Razmattaz'
s = ''.join(sorted(set(s), key = s.index))
print(s)
```

```
lst = ['R', 'a', 'a', 'z', 'm', 'a', 't', 't', 'a', 'z']
lst = list(sorted(set(lst), key = lst.index))
print(lst)
tpl = ('R', 'a', 'a', 'z', 'm', 'a', 't', 't', 'a', 'z')
tpl = tuple(sorted(set(tpl), key = tpl.index))
print(tpl)
```

Output

```
Razmt
['R', 'a', 'z', 'm', 't']
('R', 'a', 'z', 'm', 't')
```

(h)　Which operator is used for determining whether a set is a subset of another set?

Answer

The '<' operator is used to determine whether a set is a subset of another set. Corresponding method is **issubset( )**, which gives the same result.

```
s = {12, 15, 13, 23, 22, 16, 17}
t = {13, 15, 22}
print(t.issubset(s))        # print True
print(t < s)                # print True
```

(i)　What will be the output of the following program?

```
s = {'Mango', 'Banana', 'Guava', 'Kiwi'}
s.clear( )
print(s)
del(s)
print(s)
```

Program

```
set( )
NameError: name 's' is not defined
```

(j)　Which of the following is the correct way to create an empty set?

```
s1 = set( )
s2 = { }
```

What are the types of **s1** and **s2**? How will you confirm the type?

Answer

s1 = set( ) is the correct way to create an empty set.
s2 = { } is the correct way to create an empty dictionary.

Types of **s1** and **s2** can be confirmed as shown below:

```
s1 = set( )
s2 = { }
print(type(s1))
print(type(s2))
```

Its output will be:

```
<class 'set'>
<class 'dict'>
```

10 Dictionaries

[A] State whether the following statements are True or False :

(a) Dictionary elements can be accessed using position-based index.

Answer

False

(b) Dictionaries are immutable.

Answer

False

(c) **courses.clear( )** will delete the dictionary object called **courses**.

Answer

False

(d) It is possible to nest dictionaries.

Answer

True

(e) It is possible to hold multiple values against a key in a dictionary.

Answer

True

[B] Attempt the following :

(a) Write a program that reads a string from the keyboard and creates dictionary containing frequency of each character occurring in the string. Also print these occurrences in the form of a histogram.

Program

```
# Count frequency of characters in string
s = input('Enter any string: ')
freq = { }
for ch in s :
    if ch in freq :
        freq[ch] += 1
    else :
        freq[ch] = 1
print ('Count of all characters is: ', freq)

for k, v in freq.items( ) :
    print(k, ':', end = '')
    for i in range(0, v) :
```

```
      print('*', end ='')
   print( )
```

Output

```
Enter any string: Ashish Samant
Count of all characters is:  {'A': 1, 's': 2, 'h': 2, 'i': 1, ' ': 1, 'S': 1, 'a': 2,
'm': 1, 'n': 1, 't': 1}
A :*
s :**
h :**
i :*
 :*
S :*
a :**
m :*
n :*
t :*
```

(b) Create a dictionary containing names of students and marks
     obtained by them in three subjects. Write a program to replace the
     marks in three subjects with the total in three subjects, and average
     marks. Also report the topper of the class.

Program

```
# Dictionary operations
import operator
students = {
                 'Dipti' : { 'Maths' : 48, 'eng' : 60, 'hindi' : 95},
                 'Smriti' : { 'Maths' : 75,'eng' : 68,'hindi' : 89},
                 'Subodh' : { 'Maths' : 45,'eng' : 66,'hindi' : 87}
            }
tot = { }
topper_name = ''
topper_marks = 0
for nam, info in students.items( ) :
   total = 0
   for sub, marks in info.items( ) :
      total = total + marks

   avg = int(total / 3)
```

```
    students[nam] = {'Total' : total, 'Average' : avg}
    if avg > topper_marks :
      topper_name = nam
      topper_marks = avg

print(students)
print ('Topper of the class:' , topper_name)
print('Topper marks:', topper_marks)
```

Output

```
{'Dipti': {'Total': 203, 'Average': 67}, 'Smriti': {'Total': 232, 'Average':
77}, 'Subodh': {'Total': 198, 'Average': 66}}
Topper of the class: Smriti
Topper marks: 77
```

(c)   Given the following dictionary:

```
portfolio = { 'accounts' :  [ 'SBI' , 'IOB'],
              'shares' :  ['HDFC' , 'ICICI' , 'TM' , 'TCS'],
              'ornaments' : ['10 gm gold', '1 kg silver']}
```

Write a program to perform the following operations:

- Add a key to portfolio called 'MF' with values 'Reliance' and 'ABSL'.
- Set the value of 'accounts' to a list containing 'Axis' and 'BOB'.
- Sort the items in the list stored under the 'shares' key.
- Delete the list stored under 'ornaments' key.

Program

```
# Dictionary operations
portfolio = {
                'accounts' : [ 'SBI', 'IOB'],
                shares' : ['HDFC', 'ICICI', 'TM', 'TCS'],
                'ornaments' : ['10 gm gold', '1 kg silver']
            }

portfolio['MF'] = ['Reliance','ABSL']
print(portfolio)

portfolio['accounts'] = ['Axis', 'BOB']
print(portfolio)
```

```
lst = portfolio['shares']
portfolio['shares'] = sorted(lst)
print(portfolio)

del(portfolio['ornaments'])
print(portfolio)
```

Output

```
{'accounts': ['SBI', 'IOB'], 'shares': ['HDFC', 'ICICI', 'TM', 'TCS'],
'ornaments': ['10 gm gold', '1 kg silver'], 'MF': ['Reliance', 'ABSL']}
{'accounts': ['Axis', 'BOB'], 'shares': ['HDFC', 'ICICI', 'TM', 'TCS'],
'ornaments': ['10 gm gold', '1 kg silver'], 'MF': ['Reliance', 'ABSL']}
{'accounts': ['Axis', 'BOB'], 'shares': ['HDFC', 'ICICI', 'TCS', 'TM'],
'ornaments': ['10 gm gold', '1 kg silver'], 'MF': ['Reliance', 'ABSL']}
{'accounts': ['Axis', 'BOB'], 'shares': ['HDFC', 'ICICI', 'TCS', 'TM'], 'MF':
['Reliance', 'ABSL']}
```

(d) Create two dictionaries—one containing grocery items and their prices and another containing grocery items and quantity purchased. By using the values from these two dictionaries compute the total bill.

Program

```
# Calculate total bill amount
prices = { 'Bottles' : 30, 'Tiffin' : 100, 'Bag' : 400, 'Bicycle' : 2000 }
stock = { 'Bottles' : 10 , 'Tiffin' : 8, 'Bag' : 1, 'Bicycle' : 5}
total = 0
for key in prices :
    value = prices[key] * stock[key]
    total += value
print('Total Bill Amount =' , total)
```

Output

```
Bottles 300
Tiffin 800
Bag 400
Bicycle 10000
Total Bill Amount = 11500
```

(e) Which functions will you use to fetch all keys, all values and key value pairs from a given dictionary?

Answer

To fetch all keys - **keys( )**
To fetch all values - **values( )**
To fetch key value pairs - **items( )**

(f) Create a dictionary of 10 user names and passwords. Receive the user name and password from keyboard and search for them in the dictionary. Print appropriate message on the screen based on whether a match is found or not.

Program

```
# Check authentic user
users = {
            'Sanjay' : 'ceftum1250', 'Rahul' : 'Crocin100',
            'Sanket' : 'Metrogyl50', 'Shyam' : 'Miopass10',
            'Satish' : 'mvpxx_9000', 'Srishti' : 'Relaxo!',
            'Smriti' : 'newyear200', 'Sakhi' : 'Bday1711',
            'Raakhi' : 'jallosh200', 'Rahika' : 'Ultu1900'
        }
userid = input('Enter username: ')
password = input('Enter password: ')

for k, v in users.items( ) :
   if k == userid and v == password :
      print('Valid username and password')
      exit( )

print('Invalid username and password')
```

Output

```
Enter username: Smriti
Enter password: newyear200
Valid username and password
```

(g) Given the following dictionary

```
marks = { 'Subu' : { 'Maths' : 88 , 'Eng' : 60, 'SSt' : 95 },
          'Amol' : { 'Maths' : 78 , 'Eng' : 68, 'SSt' : 89 },
```

```
        'Rama' : { 'Maths' : 68 , 'Eng' : 66, 'SSt' : 87 },
        'Raka' : { 'Maths' : 56 , 'Eng' : 66, 'SSt' : 77 }}
```

Write a program to perform the following operations:

- Print marks obtained by Amol in English.
- Set marks obtained by Rama in Maths to 77.
- Sort the dictionary by name.

Program

```
marks = {
            'Subu' : { 'Maths' : 88 , 'Eng' : 60, 'SSt' : 95 },
            'Amol' : { 'Maths' : 78 , 'Eng' : 68, 'SSt' : 89 },
            'Rama' : { 'Maths' : 68 , 'Eng' : 66, 'SSt' : 87 },
            'Raka' : { 'Maths' : 56 , 'Eng' : 66, 'SSt' : 77 }
        }
print('Marks obtained by Amol in english:', marks['Amol']['Eng'])
marks['Rama']['Maths']='77'
print(marks)
marks = dict(sorted(marks.items( )))
print(marks)
```

Output

```
Marks obtained by Amol in english: 68
{'Subu': {'Maths': 88, 'Eng': 60, 'SSt': 95}, 'Amol': {'Maths': 78, 'Eng':
68, 'SSt': 89}, 'Rama': {'Maths': '77', 'Eng': 66, 'SSt': 87}, 'Raka':
{'Maths': 56, 'Eng': 66, 'SSt': 77}}
{'Amol': {'Maths': 78, 'Eng': 68, 'SSt': 89}, 'Raka': {'Maths': 56, 'Eng':
66, 'SSt': 77}, 'Rama': {'Maths': '77', 'Eng': 66, 'SSt': 87}, 'Subu':
{'Maths': 88, 'Eng': 60, 'SSt': 95}}
```

(h) Create a dictionary which stores the following data:

Interface	IP Address	status
eth0	1.1.1.1	up
eth1	2.2.2.2	up
wlan0	3.3.3.3	down
wlan1	4.4.4.4	up

Write a program to perform the following operations:

- Find the status of a given interface.
- Find interface and IP of all interfaces which are up.

- Find the total number of interfaces.
- Add two new entries to the dictionary.

Program

```python
# Working with nested directories
ifs = {
        'eth0':{'IP' : '1.1.1.1', 'Status' : 'up'},
        'eth1':{'IP' : '2.2.2.2', 'Status' : 'up'},
        'wlan0':{'IP' : '3.3.3.3', 'Status' : 'down'},
        'wlan1':{'IP' : '4.4.4.4', 'Status' : 'up'}
     }
test = input('Enter interface: ')
print(ifs[test]['Status'])

for k, v in ifs.items( ) :
   if v['Status'] == 'up' :
     print(k, v['IP'])

print('Total interfaces =', len(ifs))

ifs['eth2'] = {'IP' : '5.5.5.5', 'Status' :'down'}
ifs['wlan2'] = {'IP' : '6.6.6.6', 'Status' : 'up'}
for k, v in ifs.items( ) :
   print(k, v)
```

Output

```
Enter interface: eth1
up
eth0 1.1.1.1
eth1 2.2.2.2
wlan1 4.4.4.4
Total interfaces = 4
eth0 {'IP': '1.1.1.1', 'Status': 'up'}
eth1 {'IP': '2.2.2.2', 'Status': 'up'}
wlan0 {'IP': '3.3.3.3', 'Status': 'down'}
wlan1 {'IP': '4.4.4.4', 'Status': 'up'}
eth2 {'IP': '5.5.5.5', 'Status': 'down'}
wlan2 {'IP': '6.6.6.6', 'Status': 'up'}
```

11 Comprehensions

[A] State whether the following statements are True or False:

(a) Tuple comprehension offers a fast and compact way to generate a tuple.

Answer

True

(b) List comprehension and dictionary comprehension can be nested.

Answer

True

(c) A list being used in a list comprehension cannot be modified when it is being iterated.

Answer

True

(d) Sets being immutable cannot be used in comprehension.

Answer

False

(e) Comprehensions can be used to create a list, set or a dictionary.

Answer

True

[B] Answer the following:

(a) Write a program that generates a list of integer coordinates for all points in the first quadrant from (1, 1) to (5, 5). Use list comprehension.

Program

```
coord = [(x, y) for x in range(1, 6)for y in range(1, 6)]
print(coord)
```

Output

```
[(1, 1), (1, 2), (1, 3), (1, 4), (1, 5), (2, 1), (2, 2), (2, 3), (2, 4), (2, 5), (3, 1), (3, 2), (3, 3), (3, 4), (3, 5), (4, 1), (4, 2), (4, 3), (4, 4), (4, 5), (5, 1), (5, 2), (5, 3), (5, 4), (5, 5)]
```

(b) Using list comprehension, write a program to create a list by multiplying each element in the list by 10.

Program

```
lst = [-7, 10, 34, 2, 5, 45, 67]
lst = [(x * 10) for x in lst]
print(lst))
```

Output

```
[-70, 100, 340, 20, 50, 450, 670]
```

(c) Write a program to generate first 20 Fibonacci numbers using list comprehension.

Program

```
lst = [0, 1]
[lst.append(lst[k - 1] + lst[k - 2]) for k in range(2, 20)]
print('First 20 Fibonacci numbers:', lst)
```

Output

```
First 20 Fibonacci numbers:
[0, 1, 1, 2, 3, 5, 8, 13, 21, 34, 55, 89, 144, 233, 377, 610, 987, 1597,
2584, 4181]
```

(d) Write a program to generate two lists using list comprehension. One list should contain first 20 odd numbers and another should contain first 20 even numbers.

Program

```
lst1 = [x for x in range(40) if x % 2 != 0]
print('First 20 Odd Numbers:')
print(lst1)
lst2 = [x for x in range(40) if x % 2 == 0]
print('First 20 Even Numbers:')
print(lst2)
```

Output

```
First 20 Odd Numbers:
```

[1, 3, 5, 7, 9, 11, 13, 15, 17, 19, 21, 23, 25, 27, 29, 31, 33, 35, 37, 39]
First 20 Even Numbers:
[0, 2, 4, 6, 8, 10, 12, 14, 16, 18, 20, 22, 24, 26, 28, 30, 32, 34, 36, 38]

(e) Suppose a list contains positive and negative numbers. Write a program to create two lists—one containing positive numbers and another containing negative numbers.

Program

```
lst = [1, 2, 5, -11, -9, 10, 13, 15, -17, -19, -21, -23, 25, 27, -29]
pos = [num for num in lst if num > 0]
print(pos)
neg = [num for num in lst if num < 0]
print(neg)
```

Output

```
[1, 2, 5, 10, 13, 15, 25, 27]
[-11, -9, -17, -19, -21, -23, -29]
```

(f) Suppose a list contains 5 strings. Write a program to convert all these strings to uppercase.

Program

```
lst = ['abc', 'def', 'ghi', 'jkl', 'lmn']
lst = [s.upper( ) for s in lst]
print(lst)
```

Output

```
['ABC', 'DEF', 'GHI', 'JKL', 'LMN']
```

(g) Write a program that converts list of temperatures in Fahrenheit degrees to equivalent Celsius degrees using list comprehension.

Program

```
farh = [101, 120, 100, 67, 32]
celsius = [(e - 32) * 5 / 9 for e in farh]
print(celsius)
```

Output

[38, 48, 37, 19, 0]

(h) Write a program to generate a 2D matrix of size 4 x 5 containing random multiples of 4 in the range 40 to 160.

Program

```
import random
rows, cols = (5, 4)
arr = [[(4 * random.randint(10, 40)) for i in range(cols)] for j in range(rows)]
print(arr)
```

Output

[[72, 108, 92, 148], [88, 152, 76, 96], [148, 108, 104, 136], [132, 48, 160, 116], [140, 40, 104, 48]]

(i) Write a program that converts words present in a list into uppercase and stores them in a set.

Program

```
lst = ['function', 'office', 'type', 'product', 'most']
s = set([word.upper( ) for word in lst])
print(s)
```

Output

{'MOST', 'TYPE', 'FUNCTION', 'OFFICE', 'PRODUCT'}

12 Functions

[A] Answer the following:

(a) Write a program that defines a function **count_lower_upper( )** that accepts a string and calculates the number of uppercase and lowercase alphabets in it. It should return these values as a dictionary. Call this function for some sample strings.

Program

```python
def count_lower_upper(s) :
    dlu = {'Lower' : 0, 'Upper' : 0}
    for ch in s :
        if ch.islower( ) :
            dlu['Lower'] += 1
        elif ch.isupper( ) :
            dlu['Upper'] += 1
    return(dlu)

d = count_lower_upper('James BOnd ')
print(d)
d = count_lower_upper('Anant Amrut Mahalle')
print(d)
```

Output

```
{'Lower': 6, 'Upper': 3}
{'Lower': 14, 'Upper': 3}
```

(b) Write a program that defines a function **compute( )** that calculates the value of n + nn + nnn + nnnn, where n is digit received by the function. Test the function for digits 4 and 7.

Program

```python
import math
def compute(n) :
    s = 0
    num = 0
    for outer in range(0, 4) :
        num = num * 10 + n
        s = s + num
    return(s)
```

```
total = compute(7)
print('The value of n + nn + nnn + nnnn is', total)
total = compute(4)
print('The value of n + nn + nnn + nnnn is', total)
```

Output

```
The value of n + nn + nnn + nnnn is  8638
The value of n + nn + nnn + nnnn is  4936
```

(c) Write a program that defines a function **create_array( )** to create and return a 3D array whose dimensions are passed to the function. Also initialize each element of this array to a value passed to the function.

Program

```
def create_array(i, j, k, num):
    l = [[[num for col in range(k)] for row in range(j)] for twods in range(i)]
    return(l)

lst = create_array(4, 3, 2, 10)
print(lst)
```

Output

```
[[[10, 10], [10, 10], [10, 10]], [[10, 10], [10, 10], [10, 10]], [[10, 10], [10, 10], [10, 10]], [[10, 10], [10, 10], [10, 10]]]
```

(d) Write a program that defines a function **create_list( )** to create and return a list which is an intersection of two lists passed to it.

Program

```
def create_list(l1, l2) :
    l3 = list(set(l1) & set(l2))
    return(l3)

lst1 = [10, 20, 30, 40, 50]
lst2 = [1 ,2, 3, 40, 10]
lst3 = create_list(lst1, lst2)
print(lst3)
```

Output

[40, 10]

(e) Write a program that defines a function **sanitize_list( )** to remove all duplicate entries from the list that it receives.

Program

```
def sanitize_list(l) :
    l = list(set(l))
    return(l)

lst = [10, 3, 30, 10, 4, 3, -5, 10, 0, -5]
lst = sanitize_list(lst)
print('List after removing duplicates: ', lst)
```

Output

List after removing duplicates: [0, 3, 4, 10, -5, 30]

(f) Which of the calls to **print_it( )** in the following program will report errors.

```
def print_it(i, a, s, *args) :
        print( )
        print(i, a, s, end = ' ')
        for var in args :
                print(var, end = ' ')

print_it(10, 3.14)
print_it(20, s = 'Hi', a = 6.28)
print_it(a = 6.28, s = 'Hello', i = 30)
print_it(40, 2.35, 'Nag', 'Mum', 10)
```

Answer

The first call

print_it(10, 3.14)

will report an error 'missing 1 required positional argument: 's''

The other 3 calls are correct.

(g) Which of the calls to **fun( )** in the following program will report errors.

```
def fun(a, *args, s = '!') :
    print(a, s)
    for i in args :
            print(i, s)


fun(10)
fun(10, 20)
fun(10, 20, 30)
fun(10, 20, 30, 40, s = '+')
```

Answer

No error. All calls are correct.

13 Recursion

[A] State whether the following statements are True or False:

(a) If a recursive function uses three variables **a**, **b** and **c**, then the same set of variables are used during each recursive call.

Answer

True

(b) Multiple copies of the recursive function are created in memory.

Answer

False

(c) A recursive function must contain at least 1 **return** statement.

Answer

True

(d) Every iteration done using a **while** or **for** loop can be replaced with recursion.

Answer

True

(e) Logics expressible in the form of themselves are good candidates for writing recursive functions.

Answer

True

(f) Tail recursion is similar to a loop.

Answer

True

[B] Answer the following:

(a) Following program calculates sum of first 5 natural numbers using tail recursion. Rewrite the function to obtain the sum using head recursion.

```
def headsum(n) :
    if n != 0 :
        s = n + headsum(n - 1)
    else :
```

```
        return 0
    return s

print('Sum of First 5 Natural numbers = ', headsum(5))
```

Program

```
def headsum(n) :
    if n != 0 :
        s = n + headsum(n - 1)
    else :
        return 0
    return s

print('Sum of First 5 Natural numbers = ', headsum(5))
```

Output

```
Sum of First 5 Natural numbers = 15
```

(b) There are three pegs labeled A, B and C. Four disks are placed on peg A. The bottom-most disk is largest, and disks go on decreasing in size with the topmost disk being smallest. The objective of the game is to move the disks from peg A to peg C, using peg B as an auxiliary peg. The rules of the game are as follows:

- Only one disk may be moved at a time, and it must be the top disk on one of the pegs.
- A larger disk should never be placed on the top of a smaller disk.

Write a program to print out the sequence in which the disks should be moved such that all disks on peg A are finally transferred to peg C.

Program

```
def move(n, sp, ap, ep) :
    if n == 1 :
        print('Move from', sp ,'to', ep)
    else :
        move(n-1, sp, ep, ap)
        move(1, sp, '', ep)
        move(n-1, ap, sp, ep)
```

```
move(4, 'A', 'B', 'C')
```

Output

```
Move from A to B
Move from A to C
Move from B to C
Move from A to B
Move from C to A
Move from C to B
Move from A to B
Move from A to C
Move from B to C
Move from B to A
Move from C to A
Move from B to C
Move from A to B
Move from A to C
Move from B to C
```

14 Functional Programming

[A] State whether the following statements are True or False:

(a) lambda function cannot be used with **reduce( )** function.

Answer

False

(b) lambda, **map( )**, **filter( )**, **reduce( )** can be combined in one single expression.

Answer

True

(c) Though functions can be assigned to variables, they cannot be called using these variables.

Program

False

(d) Functions can be passed as arguments to function and returned from function.

Program

True

(e) Functions can be built at execution time, the way lists, tuples, etc. can be.

Program

True

(f) Lambda functions are always nameless.

Program

True

[B] Using lambda, **map( )**, **filter( )** and **reduce( ) or a combination thereof to perform** the following tasks:

(a) Suppose a dictionary contains type of pet (cat, dog, etc.), name of pet and age of pet. Write a program that obtains the sum of all dog's ages.

Program

```
def fun1(d) :
   if d['Type'] == 'Dog' :
      return d['Age']
   else :
      return 0

def fun2(n) :
   if n == 0 :
      return False
   else :
      return True

dct = {
            'A101' : {'Type' : 'Cat', 'Name' : 'Tauby', 'Age' : 6 },
            'A102' : {'Type' : 'Dog', 'Name' : 'Tommy', 'Age' : 8 },
            'A103' : {'Type' : 'Dog', 'Name' : 'Tiger', 'Age' : 10 }
      }
lst2 = list(filter(fun2, list(map(fun1, list(dct.values( ))))))
print('The Sum of all Dogs ages:', sum(lst2)/len(lst2))
```

Output

The Sum of all Dogs ages: 9.0

(b) Consider the following list:

lst = [1.25, 3.22, 4.68, 10.95, 32.55, 12.54]

The numbers in the list represent radii of circles. Write a program to obtain a list of areas of these circles rounded off to two decimal places.

Program

```
lst = [1.25, 3.22, 4.68, 10.98, 32.55, 12.54]
area_lst = list(map(lambda n : round(n * n * 3.14, 2), lst))
print(area_lst)
```

Output

[4.91, 32.56, 68.77, 378.56, 3326.84, 493.77]

(c)   Consider the following lists:

nums = [10, 20, 30, 40, 50, 60, 70, 80]
strs = ['A', 'B', 'C', 'D', 'E', 'F', 'G', 'H']

Write a program to obtain a list of tuples, where each tuple contains a number from one list and a string from another, in the same order in which they appear in the original lists.

Program

```
nums = [10, 20, 30, 40, 50, 60, 70, 80]
strs = ['A', 'B', 'C', 'D', 'E', 'F', 'G', 'H']
ltpl = list(map(lambda x, y : (x, y), nums, strs))
print(ltpl)
```

Output

```
[(10, 'A'), (20, 'B'), (30, 'C'), (40, 'D'), (50, 'E'), (60, 'F'), (70, 'G'), (80, 'H')]
```

(d)   Suppose a dictionary contains names of students and marks obtained by them in an examination. Write a program to obtain a list of students who obtained more than 40 marks in the examination.

Program

```
students = {
                'Dipti' : 55, 'Smriti' :12, 'Subodh' :  45,
                'Meenal' : 33, 'Harsha' : 40 , 'Bhushan' : 42
        }
lst = filter(lambda x : x[1] >= 40, students.items( ))
print(list(lst))
```

Output

```
[('Dipti', 55), ('Subodh', 45), ('Harsha', 40), ('Bhushan', 42)]
```

(e)   Consider the following list:

lst = ['Malayalam', 'Drawing', 'madamlamadam', '1234321']

Write a program to print out those strings which are palindromes.

Program

```
lst = ['Malayalam', 'Drawing', 'madamlamadam', '1234321']
lst1 = list(filter(lambda x : (x == ''.join(reversed(x))), lst))
print(lst1)
```

Output

```
['1234321']
```

(f)   A list contains names of employees. Write a program to filter out those names whose length is more than 8 characters.

Program

```
lst = ['Parmeshwar', 'Kashmira', 'Seema', 'Roopa', 'Mahalaxmi']
lst1 = filter(lambda x : len(x) >= 8, lst)
print(list(lst1))
```

Output

```
['Parmeshwar', 'Kashmira', 'Mahalaxmi']
```

(g)   A dictionary contains following information about 5 employees:
First name
Last name
Age
Grade (Skilled, Semi-skilled, Highly-skilled)

Write a program to obtain a list of employees (first name + last name) who are Highly-skilled.

Program

```
d = {
        'Dinesh' : {'last_name' : 'Sahare', 'age' : 30, 'Grade' : 'Skilled'},
        'Ram' : {'last_name' : 'Jog', 'age' : 35, 'Grade' : 'Semi-Skilled'},
        'S.' : {'last_name' : 'Sam', 'age' : 25, 'Grade' : 'Highly-Skilled'},
        'Adi' : {'last_name' : 'Lim', 'age' : 25, 'Grade' : 'Highly-Skilled'},
        'Ann' : {'last_name' : 'Mir', 'age' : 25, 'Grade' : 'Highly-Skilled'}
    }
lst = filter(lambda x : x[1]['Grade'] == 'Highly-Skilled', d.items( ))
print(list(lst))
```

Output

[('S.', {'last_name': 'Sam', 'age': 25, 'Grade': 'Highly-Skilled'}), ('Adi', {'last_name': 'Lim', 'age': 25, 'Grade': 'Highly-Skilled'}), ('Ann', {'last_name': 'Mir', 'age': 25, 'Grade': 'Highly-Skilled'})]

(h) Consider the following list:

lst = ['Benevolent', 'Dictator', 'For', 'Life']

Write a program to obtain a string 'Benevolent Dictator For Life'.

Program

```
lst = ['Benevolent', 'Dictator', 'For', 'Life']
s = ' '.join(map(str, lst))
print(s)
```

Output

Benevolent Dictator For Life

(i) Consider the following list of students in a class.

lst = ['Rahul', 'Priya', 'Chaaya', 'Narendra', 'Prashant']

Write a program to obtain a list in which all the names are converted to uppercase.

Program

```
lst = ['Rahul', 'Priya', 'Chaaya', 'Narendra', 'Prashant']
lst1 = map(lambda x : x.upper( ), lst)
print(list(lst1))
```

Output

['RAHUL', 'PRIYA', 'CHAAYA', 'NARENDRA', 'PRASHANT']

15 Modules and Packages

[A] Answer the following:

(a) Suppose there are three modules **m1.py**, **m2.py**, **m3.py**, containing functions **f1( )**, **f2( )** and **f3( )** respectively. How will you use those functions in your program?

Program

Directory structure will be as follows:

```
module
    __init__.py
    m1.py
    m2.py
    m3.py
client.py
```

The functions can be used as shown below:

```
# client.py
import module.m1
import module.m2
import module.m3

module.m1.f1( )
module.m2.f2( )
module.m3.f3( )
```

(b) Write a program containing functions **fun1( )**, **fun2( )**, **fun3( )** and some statements. Add suitable code to the program such that you can use it as a module or a normal program.

Program

```
def fun1( ) :
    print('Inside function fun1')

def fun2( ) :
    print('Inside function fun2')

def fun3( ) :
    print('Inside function fun3')

def main( ) :
```

```
    fun1( )
    fun2( )
    fun3( )

if (__name__ == '__main__') :
    main( )
```

(c) Suppose a module **mod.py** contains functions **f1( )**, **f2( )** and **f3( )**. Write 4 forms of import statements to use these functions in your program.

Program

Directory structure will be as follows:
module
    __init__.py
    mod.py
client.py

```
# client.py - Method 1
import module.mod
module.mod.f1( )
module.mod.f2( )
module.mod.f3( )

# client.py - Method 2
from module.mod import f1
from module.mod import f2
from module.mod import f3
f1( )
f2( )
f3( )

# client.py - Method 3
from module.mod import *
f1( )
f2( )
f3( )

# client.py - Method 4
import module.mod as M
```

```
M.f1( )
M.f2( )
M.f3( )
```

[B] Attempt the following:

(d) What is the difference between a module and a package?

Answer

A module is a .py file containing function definitions and statements. So all .py files are modules.
A directory is treated as a package if it contains a file named __init__.py file in it.

(e) What is the purpose behind creating multiple packages and modules?

Answer

Multiple packages and modules are created to manage the complexity of code and to organize the code in reusable pieces.

(f) By default, to which module do the statements in a program belong? How do we access the name of this module?

Answer

By default, the statements in a program belong to __main__ module. We access the name of this module through the variable __name__.

(g) In the following statement what do **a**, **b**, **c**, **x** represent?

```
import a.b.c.x
```

Answer

a, b, c, x are nested modules.

(h) If module **m** contains a function **fun( )**, what is wrong with the following statements?

```
import m
fun( )
```

Answer

To call fun( ), we must use the syntax

m.fun( )

(i) What are the contents of **PYTHONPATH** variable? How can we access its contents programmatically?

Answer

PYTHONPATH environment variable contains a list of directories. They can be accessed through the following code snippet:

```
import sys
for p in sys.path :
    print(p)
```

(j) What does the content of **sys.path** signify? What does the order of contents of **sys.path** signify?

Answer

The **sys.path** variable contains a list of directories. The first directory in the list is the directory from where the current script has been executed. This is followed by a list of directories as specified in **PYTHONPATH** environment variable.

The modules being used in the program will be searched in the same order as the order of directories in the list.

(k) Where a list of third-party packages is maintained?

Answer

PyPI maintains a list of third-party package.

(l) Which tool is commonly used for installing third-party packages?

Answer

pip is a commonly used tool for installing third-party packages.

(m) Do the following import statements serve the same purpose?

```
# version 1
import a, b, c, d

# version 2
import a
import b
import c
import d

# version 3
from a import *
from b import *
from c import *
from d import *
```

Answer

Yes

[C] State whether the following statements are True or False:

(a) A function can belong to a module and the module can belong to a package.

Answer

True

(b) A package can contain one or more modules in it.

Answer

True

(c) Nested packages are allowed.

Answer

True

(d) Contents of **sys.path** variable cannot be modified.

Answer

False

(e) In the statement **import a.b.c**, **c** cannot be a function.

Answer

True

(f) It is a good idea to use * to import all the functions/classes defined in a module.

Answer

True

16 Namespaces

[A] State whether the following statements are True or False:

(a) Symbol table consists of information about each identifier used in our program.

Answer

True

(b) An identifier with global scope can be used anywhere in the program.

Answer

True

(c) It is possible to define a function within another function.

Answer

True

(d) If a function is nested inside another function then variables defined in outer function are available to inner function.

Answer

True

(e) If nested functions create two variables with same name, then the two variables are treated as same variable.

Answer

False

(f) An inner function can be called from outside the outer function.

Answer

False

(g)   If a function creates a variable by the same name as the one that exists in global scope, the function's variable will shadow out the global variable.

Answer

True

(h)   Variables defined at global scope are available to all the functions defined in the program.

Answer

True

[B]   Answer the following:

(a)   What is the difference between the function **locals( )** and **globals( )**?

Answer

locals( ) - When called from a function/method, it returns a dictionary of identifiers that are accessible from that function/method.

globals( ) - When called from a function/method, it returns a dictionary of global identifiers that can be accessible from that function/method.

(b)   Would the output of the following print statements be same or different?

```
a = 20
b = 40
print(globals( ))
print(locals( ))
```

Answer

Output will be same.

(c) Which different scopes can an identifier have?

Answer

Local(L), Enclosing(E), Global(G), Built-in(B).

(d) Which is the most liberal scope that an identifier can have?

Answer

Global scope is the most liberal scope that an identifier can have.

17 Classes and Objects

[A] State whether the following statements are True or False:

(a) Class attributes and object attributes are same.

Answer

False

(b) A class data member is useful when all objects of the same class must share a common item of information.

Answer

True

(c) If a class has a data member and three objects are created from this class, then each object would have its own data member.

Answer

True

(d) A class can have class data as well as class methods.

Answer

True

(e) Usually data in a class is kept private and the data is accessed / manipulated through object methods of the class.

Answer

True

(f) Member functions of an object have to be called explicitly, whereas, the **__init__( )** method gets called automatically.

Answer

True

(g) A constructor gets called whenever an object gets instantiated.

Answer

True

(h)   The **__init__( )** method never returns a value.

Answer

True

(i)   When an object goes out of scope, its **__del__( )** method gets called automatically.

Answer

True

(j)   The **self** variable always contains the address of the object using which the method/data is being accessed.

Answer

True

(k)   The **self** variable can be used even outside the class.

Answer

False

(l)   The **__init__( )** method gets called only once during the lifetime of an object.

Answer

True

(m) By default, instance data and methods in a class are public.

Answer

True

(n)   In a class 2 constructors can coexist—a 0-argument constructor and a 2-argument constructor.

Answer

True

[B] Answer the following:

(a) Which methods in a class act as constructor?

Answer

__init__( ) in a class acts as a constructor.

(b) How many objects are created in the following code snippet?

```
a = 10
b = a
c = b
```

Answer

One object is created in the above code snippet.

(c) What is the difference between variables, **age** and **_age**?

Answer

age is a public attribute but _age is a private attribute of an object.

(d) What is the difference between the function **vars( )** and **dir( )**?

Answer

vars( ) - Returns a dictionary of attributes and their values.
dir( ) - Returns a list of attributes.

(e) What is the purpose of built-in functions **dir( )**, **vars( )**, **global( )** and **local( )**?

Answer

vars( ) - It returns a dictionary of attributes and their values. It can return an object's class's attributes, and recursively the attributes of its class's base classes.

dir( ) - It returns a list of attributes. It can return an object's attributes, object's class's attributes and recursively the attributes of its class's base classes.

globals( ) - It returns a dictionary of global identifiers that can be accessible from a function/method.

locals( ) - It returns a dictionary of identifiers that are accessible from that function/method.

(f)   What will be the output of the following program?

```
var = 1.1
print(var)

def fun( ) :
    var = 2.2
    print(var)

fun( )
print(var)
```

Output

```
1.1
2.2
1.1
```

[C] Attempt the following:

(a)   Write a program to create a class that represents Complex numbers containing real and imaginary parts and then use it to perform complex number addition, subtraction, multiplication and division.

Program

```
import math

class Complex( ) :
    def __init__(self, x, y) :
        self.real = x
        self.imag = y
```

```python
  def display(self) :
    print(self.real, '+', self.imag, 'i')

  def add(self, x) :
    r = self.real + x.real
    i = self.imag + x.imag
    return Complex(r, i)

  def subtract(self, x) :
    r = self.real - x.real
    i = self.imag - x.imag
    return Complex(r, i)

  def multiply(self, x) :
    r = self.real * x.real - self.imag * x.imag
    i = self.real * x.imag + self.imag * x.real
    return Complex(r, i)

  def conj(self) :
    r = self.real
    i = -self.imag
    return Complex(r, i)

  def mods(self) :
    mod2 = self.real * self.real + self.imag * self.imag
    return math.sqrt(mod2)

  def divide(self, x) :
    m = x.mods( )
    c = x.conj( )
    if m == 0 :
      print('Unable to divide the complex numbers')
    else :
      quo = self.multiply(c)
      quo.real = quo.real / m
      quo.imag = quo.imag / m
      return quo

a = Complex(2, 3)
b = Complex(6, -1)
print('a: ', end = '')
```

```
a.display( )
print('b: ', end = '')
b.display( )

c = a.add(b)
print('a + b = ', end = '')
c.display( )
d = a.subtract(b)
print('a - b = ', end = '')
d.display( )
e = a.multiply(b)
print('a * b = ', end = '')
e.display( )
f = a.divide ( b )
print('a / b = ', end = '')
f.display( )
```

Output

```
a: 2 + 3 i
b: 6 + -1 i
a + b = 8 + 2 i
a - b = -4 + 4 i
a * b = 15 + 16 i
a / b = 1.4795908857482156 + 3.287979746107146 i
```

(b) Write a program that implements a **Matrix** class and performs addition, multiplication, and transpose operations on 3 x 3 matrices.

Program

```
class Matrix :
    size = 3
    def __init__(self, r, c) :
        self.rows = r
        self.cols = c
        self.arr = [ ]

    def initializeMatrix(self) :
        print('Enter the contents of the matrix row-wise: ')
```

```python
    for i in range(self.rows) :
      print('Row ', i, ':')
      a = [ ]
      for j in range(self.cols) :
        a.append(int(input( )))
      print('Row ', i, 'completed.')
      self.arr.append(a)
    print('Matrix initialized successfully.')

  def displayMatrix(self) :
    for i in range(self.rows) :
      for j in range(self.cols) :
        print('{0:<5}'.format(self.arr[i][j]), end = '')
      print( )

  def add(self, m) :
    mat = Matrix(self.rows, self.cols)
    for i in range(self.rows) :
      lst = [ ]
      for j in range(self.cols) :
        lst.append(self.arr[i][j] + m.arr[i][j])
      mat.arr.append(lst)
    return mat


  def multiply(self, m) :
    mat = Matrix(self.rows, m.cols)
    for i in range(self.rows) :
      lst = [ ]
      for j in range(self.cols) :
        temp = 0
        for k in range(self.cols) :
          temp = temp + self.arr[i][k] * m.arr[k][j]
        lst.append(temp)
      mat.arr.append(lst)
    return mat

  def transpose(self) :
    mat = Matrix(self.cols, self.rows)
    for i in range(self.cols) :
      lst = [ ]
```

```python
                        for j in range(self.rows) :
                            lst.append(self.arr[j][i])
                        mat.arr.append(lst)
                return mat

print('Initialize Matrix 1:')
mat1 = Matrix(3, 3)
mat1.initializeMatrix( )

print('Initialize Matrix 2:')
mat2 = Matrix(3, 3)
mat2.initializeMatrix( )

print('First Matrix: ')
mat1.displayMatrix( )

print('Second Matrix: ')
mat2.displayMatrix( )

mat3 = mat1.add(mat2)
print('After addition: ')
mat3.displayMatrix( )

mat4 = mat1.multiply(mat2)
print('After multiplication: ')
mat4.displayMatrix( )

mat5 = mat1.transpose( )
print('Transpose of Matrix 1: ')
mat5.displayMatrix( )
```

Output

```
Initialize Matrix 1:
Enter the contents of the matrix row-wise:
Row  0 :
1
2
3
Row  0 completed.
Row  1 :
1
```

```
2
3
Row  1 completed.
Row  2 :
1
2
3
Row  2 completed.
Matrix initialized successfully.
Initialize Matrix 2:
Enter the contents of the matrix row-wise:
Row  0 :
1
1
1
Row  0 completed.
Row  1 :
1
1
1
Row  1 completed.
Row  2 :
1
1
1
Row  2 completed.
Matrix initialized successfully.
First Matrix:
1   2   3
1   2   3
1   2   3
Second Matrix:
1   1   1
1   1   1
1   1   1
After addition:
2   3   4
2   3   4
2   3   4
After multiplication:
6   6   6
```

```
6  6  6
6  6  6
Transpose of Matrix 1:
1  1  1
2  2  2
3  3  3
```

(c) Write a program to create a class that can calculate the surface area and volume of a solid. The class should also have a provision to accept the data relevant to the solid.

Program

```
class Solid :
    def __init__(self, len_cbd = 0, br_cbd = 0, ht_cbd = 0, side_cube =
                    0, ht_cyl = 0, rad_cyl = 0, rad_sphere = 0) :
        self.len_cbd = len_cbd
        self.br_cbd = br_cbd
        self.ht_cbd = ht_cbd
        self.side_cube = side_cube
        self.ht_cyl = ht_cyl
        self.rad_cyl = rad_cyl
        self.rad_sphere = rad_sphere

    def sarea_cuboid(self) :
        sa = 2 * (self.len_cbd * self.br_cbd + self.len_cbd * self.ht_cbd
                    + self.ht_cbd * self.br_cbd)
        print('Surface area of cuboid is:', sa)

    def vol_cuboid(self) :
        v = self.len_cbd * self.br_cbd * self.ht_cbd
        print('Volume of cuboid is:', v)

    def sarea_cube(self) :
        sa = 6 * (self.side_cube * self.side_cube)
        print('Surface area of cube is:', sa)

    def vol_cube(self) :
        v = self.side_cube * self.side_cube * self.side_cube
        print('Volume of cube is:', v)

    def sarea_cyl(self) :
```

```python
      sa = 2 * (3.14 * self.rad_cyl * self.ht_cyl + 3.14 * self.rad_cyl
            * self.rad_cyl)
      print('Surface area of cylinder is:', sa)

   def vol_cyl(self) :
      v =  3.14 * self.rad_cyl * self.rad_cyl * self.ht_cyl
      print('Volume of cylinder is:', v)

   def sarea_sphere(self) :
      sa = 4 * (3.14 * self.rad_sphere * self.rad_sphere)
      print('Surface area of sphere is:', sa)

   def vol_sphere(self) :
      v =  4 / 3 * 3.14 * self.rad_sphere * self.rad_sphere
            * self.rad_sphere
      print('Volume of sphere is:', v)

choice = 1
while choice != 0 :
   print('1. Cuboid')
   print('2. Cube')
   print('3. Cylinder')
   print('4. Sphere')
   print('0. Exit')
   choice = int(input('Enter choice: '))

   if choice == 1 :
      l = int(input('Length of cuboid: '))
      b = int(input('Breadth of cuboid: '))
      h = int(input('Height of cuboid: '))
      s = Solid(len_cbd = l, br_cbd = b, ht_cbd = h)
      s.sarea_cuboid( )
      s.vol_cuboid( )

   elif choice == 2 :
      sd = int(input('Side of cube: '))
      s = Solid(side_cube = sd)
      s.sarea_cube( )
      s.vol_cube( )

   elif choice == 3 :
```

```
            h = int(input('Height of cylinder: '))
            r = int(input('Radius of base: '))
            s = Solid(rad_cyl = r, ht_cyl = h)
            s.sarea_cyl( )
            s.vol_cyl( )

        elif choice == 4 :
            r = int(input('Radius of sphere: '))
            s = Solid(rad_sphere = r)
            s.sarea_sphere( )
            s.vol_sphere( )

        elif choice == 0 :
            print('Exiting!')

        else :
            print('Invalid choice!!')
```

Output

```
1. Cuboid
2. Cube
3. Cylinder
4. Sphere
0. Exit
Enter choice: 1
Length of cuboid: 5
Breadth of cuboid: 4
Height of cuboid: 3
Surface area of cuboid is :  94
Volume of cuboid is :  60
1. Cuboid
2. Cube
3. Cylinder
4. Sphere
0. Exit
Enter choice: 2
Side of cube: 5
Surface area of cube is :  150
Volume of cube is :  125
1. Cuboid
2. Cube
```

```
3. Cylinder
4. Sphere
0. Exit
Enter choice: 3
Height of cylinder: 6
Radius of base: 3
Surface area of cylinder is :  169.56
Volume of cylinder is :  169.56
1. Cuboid
2. Cube
3. Cylinder
4. Sphere
0. Exit
Enter choice: 4
Radius of sphere: 6
Surface area of sphere is :  452.15999999999997
Volume of sphere is :  904.3199999999998
1. Cuboid
2. Cube
3. Cylinder
4. Sphere
0. Exit
Enter choice: 8
Invalid choice!!
1. Cuboid
2. Cube
3. Cylinder
4. Sphere
0. Exit
Enter choice: 0
Exiting!
```

(d) Write a program to create a class that can calculate the perimeter / circumference and area of a regular shape. The class should also have a provision to accept the data relevant to the shape.

Program

```python
class Shape :
    def __init__(self, len_rect = 0, br_rect = 0, side_square = 0,
rad_cir = 0) :
        self.len_rect = len_rect
```

```python
            self.br_rect = br_rect
            self.side_square = side_square
            self.rad_cir = rad_cir

        def area_rect(self) :
            a = self.len_rect * self.br_rect
            print('Area of rectangle is:', a)

        def peri_rect(self) :
            p = 2 * (self.len_rect + self.br_rect)
            print('Perimeter of rectangle is:', p)

        def area_square(self) :
            a = self.side_square * self.side_square
            print('Area of square is:', a)

        def peri_square(self) :
            p = 4 * self.side_square
            print('Perimeter of square is:', p)

        def area_cir(self) :
            a = 3.14 * self.rad_cir * self.rad_cir
            print('Area of cicle is:', a)

        def peri_cir(self) :
            p =  2 * 3.14 * self.rad_cir
            print('Perimeter of circle is:', p)

choice = 1
while choice != 0 :
    print('1. Rectangle')
    print('2. Square')
    print('3. Circle')
    print('0. Exit')
    choice = int(input('Enter choice: '))

    if choice == 1 :
        l = int(input('Length of rectangle: '))
        b = int(input('Breadth of rectangle: '))
        s = Shape(len_rect = l, br_rect = b)
        s.area_rect( )
```

```python
        s.peri_rect( )

    elif choice == 2 :
        sd = int(input('Side of square: '))
        s = Shape(side_square = sd)
        s.area_square( )
        s.peri_square( )

    elif choice == 3 :
        r = int(input('Radius of circle: '))
        s = Shape(rad_cir = r)
        s.area_cir( )
        s.peri_cir( )

    elif choice == 0 :
        print('Exiting!')

    else :
        print('Invalid choice!!')
```

Output

```
1. Rectangle
2. Square
3. Circle
0. Exit
Enter choice: 1
Length of rectangle: 6
Breadth of rectangle: 5
Area of rectangle is: 30
Perimeter of rectangle is: 22
1. Rectangle
2. Square
3. Circle
0. Exit
Enter choice: 2
Side of square: 4
Area of square is: 16
Perimeter of square is: 16
1. Rectangle
2. Square
3. Circle
```

```
0. Exit
Enter choice: 3
Radius of circle: 5
Area of cicle is: 78.5
Perimeter of circle is: 31.400000000000002
1. Rectangle
2. Square
3. Circle
0. Exit
Enter choice: 5
Invalid choice!!
1. Rectangle
2. Square
3. Circle
0. Exit
Enter choice: 0
Exiting!
```

(e) Write a program that creates and uses a **Time** class to perform various time arithmetic operations.

Program

```python
class Time :
    def __init__(self, hr = 0, mnt = 0, sec  = 0) :
        self.hours = hr
        self.minutes = mnt
        self.seconds  = sec

    def add_seconds(self, sec) :
        if sec > 86400 :
            return 1

        h = int(sec / 3600)
        m = int((sec - h * 3600) / 60)
        s = int((sec - h * 3600 - m * 60))

        self.hours = self.hours + h
        self.minutes = self.minutes + m
        self.seconds = self.seconds + s
        if self.seconds >= 60 :
            self.minutes += 1
```

```python
            self.seconds -= 60
        if self.minutes >= 60 :
            self.hours += 1
            self.minute -= 60
        if self.hours >= 24 :
            self.hours = self.hours % 24

    def sub_seconds(self, sec) :
        if sec > 86400 :
            return 1

        h = int(sec / 3600)
        m = int((sec - h * 3600) / 60)
        s = int((sec - h * 3600 - m * 60))

        self.hours = self.hours - h
        self.minutes = self.minutes - m
        self.seconds = self.seconds - s
        if self.seconds < 0 :
            self.minutes -= 1
            self.seconds = 60 + self.seconds
        if self.minutes < 0 :
            self.hours -= 1
            self.minutes = 60 + self.minutes
        if self.hours < 0 :
            self.hours = 24 + self.hours

    def display(self) :
        print(self.hours, ':', self.minutes, ':', self.seconds)

t1 = Time(10, 15, 35)
print('Original time = ', end ='')
t1.display( )
val = t1.add_seconds(144)
if val == 1 :
    print('Cannot add more than 24 hours')
else :
    print('Time after adding 144 seconds = ', end ='')
    t1.display( )

print('Original time = ', end ='')
```

```
t1.display( )
val = t1.add_seconds(4000)
if val == 1 :
   print('Cannot add more than 24 hours')
else :
   print('Time after adding 4000 seconds = ', end ='')
   t1.display( )

print('Original time = ', end ='')
t1.display( )
val = t1.sub_seconds(4000)
if val == 1 :
   print('Cannot deduct more than 24 hours')
else :
   print('Time after deducting 4000 seconds = ', end ='')
   t1.display( )

print('Original time = ', end ='')
t1.display( )
val = t1.sub_seconds(144)
if val == 1 :
   print('Cannot deduct more than 24 hours')
else :
   print('Time after deducting 144 seconds = ', end ='')
   t1.display( )
```

Output

```
Original time = 10 : 15 : 35
Time after adding 144 seconds = 10 : 17 : 59
Original time = 10 : 17 : 59
Time after adding 4000 seconds = 11 : 24 : 39
Original time = 11 : 24 : 39
Time after deducting 4000 seconds = 10 : 17 : 59
Original time = 10 : 17 : 59
Time after deducting 144 seconds = 10 : 15 : 35
```

(f) Write a program to implement a linked list data structure by creating a linked list class. Each node in the linked list should contain name of the car, its price and a link to the next node.

Program

```python
class Node:
  def __init__(self, car, price):
    self.car = car
    self.price = price
    self.next = None

class LinkedList:
  def __init__(self):
    self.head = None

  def add(self, c, pr):
    n = Node(c, pr)
    if self.head is None :
      self.head = n
    else :
      p = self.head
      while p.next is not None :
          p = p.next

      p.next = n

  def display(self):
    p = self.head
    while p is not None:
        print(p.car, p.price)
        p = p.next

llst = LinkedList( )
llst.add('BMW', '55 lac')
llst.add('Honda City', '12 lac')
llst.add('Mercedes', '75 lac')
llst.add('Esteem', '10 lac')
llst.add('i20', '6 lac')
llst.add('i10', '4 lac')
llst.display( )
```

Output

```
BMW 55 lac
Honda City 12 lac
```

Mercedes 75 lac
Esteem 10 lac
i20 6 lac
i10 4 lac

[D] Match the following:

a. dir( )   1. Nested packages
b. vars( )   2. Identifiers, their type & scope
c. Variables in a function   3. Returns dictionary
d. import a.b.c   4. Local namespace
e. Symbol table   5. Returns list
f. Variables outside all functions   6. Global namespace

Answer

dir( ) - Returns list
vars( ) - Returns dictionary
Variables in a function - Local namespace
import a.b.c - Nested packages
Symbol table - Identifiers, their type & scope
Variables outside all functions - Global namespace

18 Intricacies of Classes & Objects

[A] State whether the following statements are True or False:

(a) A global function can call a class method as well as an instance method.

Answer

True

(b) In Python a function, class, method and module are treated as objects.

Answer

True

(c) Given an object, it is possible to determine its type and address.

Answer

True

(d) It is possible to delete attributes of an object during execution of the program.

Answer

True

[B] Answer the following:

(a) Which functions should be defined to overload the +, -, / and // operators?

Answer

```
+    __add__(self, other)
-    __sub__(self, other)
/    __truediv__(self, other)
//   __floordiv__(self, other)
```

(b) How many objects are created by lst = [10, 10, 10, 30]?

Answer

Two objects are created, one which refers to 10 and another which refers to 30. This can be verified as follows:

```
lst = [10, 10, 10, 30]
print(id(lst[0]), id(lst[1]), id(lst[2]), id(lst[3]))
```

Its output will be:

```
1481758656 1481758656 1481758656 1481758976
```

(c) How will you define a structure **Employee** containing the attributes Name, Age, Salary, Address, Hobbies dynamically?

Answer

```
class Employee:
    pass
e = Employee( )
e.name = 'Rohan'
e.age = 29
e.salary = 340000
e.address = 'xyz'
e.hobbies = 'painting'
```

[C] Match the following:

a. Can't use as identifier name	1. class name
b. basic_salary	2. class variable
c. CellPhone	3. keyword
d. count	4. local variable in a function
e. self	5. private variable
f. _fuel_used	6. strongly private identifier
g. __draw( )	7. method that Python calls
h. __iter__( )	8. meaningful only in instance func.

Answer

```
Can't use as identifier name - keyword
basic_salary - class variable
CellPhone - class name
count - local variable in a function
self - meaningful only in instance function
_fuel_used - private variable
```

__draw( ) - strongly private identifier
__iter__( ) - method that Python calls

19 Containership and Inheritance

137

[A] State whether the following statements are True or False:

(a) Inheritance is the ability of a class to inherit properties and behavior from a parent class by extending it.

Answer

True

(b) Containership is the ability of a class to contain objects of different classes as member data.

Answer

True

(c) We can derive a class from a base class even if the base class's source code is not available.

Answer

True

(d) Multiple inheritance is different from multiple levels of inheritance.

Answer

True

(e) An object of a derived class cannot access members of base class if the member names begin with __.

Answer

True

(f) Creating a derived class from a base class requires fundamental changes to the base class.

Answer

False

(g)　If a base class contains a member function **func( )**, and a derived class does not contain a function with this name, an object of the derived class cannot access **func( )**.

Answer

False

(h)　If no constructors are specified for a derived class, objects of the derived class will use the constructors in the base class.

Answer

False

(i)　If a base class and a derived class each include a member function with the same name, the member function of the derived class will be called by an object of the derived class.

Answer

True

(j)　A class **D** can be derived from a class **C**, which is derived from a class **B**, which is derived from a class **A**.

Answer

True

(k)　It is illegal to make objects of one class members of another class.

Answer

False

[B]　Answer the following:

(a)　Which module should be imported to create abstract class?

Answer

abc

(b)　For a class to be abstract from which class should we inherit it?

Answer

ABC

(c) Implement a **String** class containing the following functions:

   –   Overloaded += operator function to perform string concatenation.
   –   Method **toLower( )** to convert upper case letters to lower case.
   –   Method **toUpper( )** to convert lower case letters to upper case.

Program

```python
class MyString :
   def __init__(self, s = '') :
      self.s = s

   def display(self) :
      print(self.s)

   def toLower(self) :
      self.s = self.s.lower( )

   def toUpper(self) :
      self.s = self.s.upper( )

   def __iadd__(self, other) :
      self.s = self.s + other.s
      return MyString(self.s)

s1 = MyString('Hello')
s1.display( )
s1.toLower( )
s1.display( )
s1.toUpper( )
s1.display( )
s2 = MyString('Good Morning')
s1 += s2
s1.display( )
```

Output

Hello

```
hello
HELLO
HELLOGood Morning
```

(d)　Suppose there is a base class **B** and a derived class **D** derived from **B**. **B** has two **public** member functions **b1( )** and **b2( )**, whereas **D** has two member functions **d1( )** and **d2( )**. Write these classes for the following different situations:

- **b1( )** should be accessible from main module, **b2( )** should not be.
- Neither **b1( )**, nor **b2( )** should be accessible from main module.
- Both **b1( )** and **b2( )** should be accessible from main module.

Program

```python
# Version 1: b1( ) accessible, b2( ) inaccessible
class B :
   def b1(self) :
     print('B - b1')

   def __b2(self) :
     print('B - b2')

class D(B) :
   def d1(self) :
     print('D - d1')

   def d2(self) :
     print('D - d2')

b = B( )
b.b1( )      # works
b.__b2( )  # error


# Version 2: b1( ) inaccessible, b2( ) inaccessible
class B :
   def __b1(self) :
     print('B - b1')

   def __b2(self) :
     print('B - b2')
```

```
class D(B) :
  def d1(self) :
    print('D - d1')

  def d2(self) :
    print('D - d2')

b = B( )
b.__b1( )  # error
b.__b2( )  # error


# Version 3: b1( ) accessible, b2( ) accessible
class B :
  def b1(self) :
    print('B - b1')

  def b2(self) :
    print('B - b2')

class D(B) :
  def d1(self) :
    print('D - d1')

  def d2(self) :
    print('D - d2')

b = B( )
b.b1( )      # works
b.b2( )      # works
```

(e) If a class **D** is derived from two base classes **B1** and **B2**, then write
     these classes each containing a constructor. Ensure that while
     building an object of type **D**, constructor of **B2** should get called.
     Also provide a destructor in each class. In what order would these
     destructors get called?

Program

```
class B1 :
  def __init__(self) :
```

```python
      print('B1 Ctor')

  def __del__(self) :
    print('B1 Dtor')

class B2 :
  def __init__(self) :
    print('B2 Ctor')

  def __del__(self) :
    print('B2 Dtor')

class D(B1, B2) :
  def __init__(self) :
    B2.__init__(self)
    print('D Ctor')

  def __del__(self) :
    B1.__del__(self)
    B2.__del__(self)
    print('D Dtor')

d = D( )
d = None
```

Output

```
B2 Ctor
D Ctor
B1 Dtor
B2 Dtor
D Dtor
```

The destructors of base classes get called before destructor of derived class.

(f)   Create an abstract class called **Vehicle** containing methods **speed( )**, **maintenance( )** and **value( )** in it. Derive classes **FourWheeler**, **TwoWheeler** and **Airborne** from **Vehicle** class. Check whether you are able to prevent creation of objects of **Vehicle** class. Call the methods using objects of other classes.

Program

```python
from abc import ABC, abstractmethod
class Vehicle(ABC) :
  @abstractmethod
  def speed(self) :
    pass

  def maintenance(self) :
    pass

  def value(self) :
    pass

class FourWheeler(Vehicle) :
  def speed(self) :
    print('In FourWheeler.speed')

  def maintenance(self) :
    print('In FourWheeler.maintenance')

  def value(self) :
    print('In FourWheeler.value')

class TwoWheeler(Vehicle) :
  def speed(self) :
    print('In TwoWheeler.speed')

  def maintenance(self) :
    print('In TwoWheeler.maintenance')

  def value(self) :
    print('In TwoWheeler.value')

# v = Vehicle( )   # will result in error, as Vehicle is abstract class

fw = FourWheeler( )
fw.speed( )
fw.maintenance( )
fw.value( )

tw = TwoWheeler( )
```

```
tw.speed( )
tw.maintenance( )
tw.value( )
```

Output

```
In FourWheeler.speed
In FourWheeler.maintenance
In FourWheeler.value
In TwoWheeler.speed
In TwoWheeler.maintenance
In TwoWheeler.value
```

(g)　Assume a class **D** that is derived from class **B**. Which of the following can an object of class **D** access?

- members of **D**
- members of **B**

Answer

Both

[C]　Match the following:

a. __mro__( )	1. 'has a' relationship
b. Inheritance	2. Object creation not allowed
c. __var	3. Super class
d. Abstract class	4. Root class
e. Parent class	5. 'is a' relationship
f. object	6. Name mangling
g. Child class	7. Decides resolution order
h. Containership	8. Sub class

Answer

__mro__( ) - Decides resolution order
Inheritance - 'is a' relationship
__var - Name mangling
Abstract class - Object creation not allowed
Parent class - Super class
object - Root class
Child class - Sub class
Containership - 'has a' relationship

20 Iterators and Generators

147

[A] Answer the following:

(a) Write a program to create a list of 5 odd integers. Replace the third element with a list of 4 even integers. Flatten, sort and print the list.

Program

```
lst = [1, 3, 9, 13, 17]
lst[2] = [2, 8, 12, 16]
lst1 = [ ]
for num in lst[2] :
    lst1.append(num)
lst = lst[0:2] + lst1 + lst[3:]
print(lst)
```

Output

```
[1, 3, 2, 8, 12, 16, 13, 17]
```

(b) Write a program to flatten the following list:

```
mat1 = [[1, 2, 3, 4], [5, 6, 7, 8], [9, 10, 11, 12]]
```

Program

```
lst = [ ]
mat1 = [[1, 2, 3, 4], [5, 6, 7, 8], [9, 10, 11, 12]]
lst = [ ]
for m in mat1 :
    for ele in m :
        lst.append(ele)
print(lst)
```

Output

```
[1, 2, 3, 4, 5, 6, 7, 8, 9, 10, 11, 12]
```

(c) Write a program to generate a list of numbers in the range 2 to 50 that are divisible by 2 and 4.

Program

```
lst = [n for n in range(2, 50) if n % 2 == 0 and n % 4 == 0]
print(lst)
```

Output

[4, 8, 12, 16, 20, 24, 28, 32, 36, 40, 44, 48]

(d) Suppose there are two lists, each holding 5 strings. Write a program to generate a list that consists of strings that are concatenated by picking corresponding elements from the two lists.

Program

```
lst1 = ['Cat', 'Dog', 'Lion', 'Tiger']
lst2 = ['Lily', 'Rose', 'Hibiscus', 'Lavender']
loft = zip(lst1, lst2)
lst3 = [ ]
for tpl in loft :
    lst3.append(tpl[0] + tpl[1])
print(lst3)
```

Output

['CatLily', 'DogRose', 'LionHibiscus', 'TigerLavender']

(e) Suppose a list contains 20 integers generated randomly. Receive a number from the keyboard and report position of all occurrences of this number in the list.

Program

```
import random
lst =[int(10 * random.random( )) for n in range(20)]
print(lst)
num = int(input('Enter number between 1 to 10: '))
indexlist = [i for i in range(len(lst)) if lst[i] == num]
print(num, 'is present at following positions')
print(indexlist)
```

Output

```
[2, 8, 1, 6, 0, 6, 4, 4, 4, 8, 6, 9, 1, 2, 5, 0, 1, 4, 8, 8]
Enter number between 1 to 10: 4
4 is present at following positions
[6, 7, 8, 17]
```

(f)   Suppose there are two lists—one contains questions and another contains lists of 4 possible answers for each question. Write a program to generate a list that contains lists of question and its 4 possible answers.

Program

```
qlist = ['What is capital of India', 'Which is your favorite color?']
alist = [['Delhi', 'Mumbai', 'Hyderabad', 'Bangalore'], ['Red', 'Blue',
'White', 'Black']]
qalist = [ ]
for q, a in zip(qlist, alist) :
    lst = [q, *a]
    qalist.append(lst)
print(qalist)
```

Output

```
[['What is capital of India', 'Delhi', 'Mumbai', 'Hyderabad',
'Bangalore'], ['Which is your favorite color?', 'Red', 'Blue', 'White',
'Black']]
```

(g)   Suppose a list has 20 numbers. Write a program that removes all duplicates from this list.

Program

```
lst =[1, 1, 1, 1, 1, 2, 2, 2, 3, 1, 4, 1, 3, 2, 1, 1, 2, 2, 5, 5]
lst = list(set(lst))
print(lst)
```

Output

```
[1, 2, 3, 4, 5]
```

(h)   Write a program to obtain a median value of a list of numbers, without disturbing the order of the numbers in the list.

Program

```
lst1 = [1, 2, 3, 4, 5, 6]
n = len(lst1)
s = sorted(lst1)
```

```
m = (sum(s[n // 2 - 1 : n // 2 + 1]) / 2.0, s[n // 2])[n % 2]
print(m)

lst2 = [7, 6, 5, 4, 3, 2, 1]
n = len(lst2)
s = sorted(lst2)
m = (sum(s[n // 2 - 1 : n // 2 + 1]) / 2.0, s[n // 2])[n % 2]
print(m)
```

Output

```
3.5
4
```

(i) A list contains only positive and negative integers. Write a program to obtain the number of negative numbers present in the list.

Program

```
lst1 = [-1, -2, -3, 1, 2, 3]
lst2 = [n for n in lst1 if n < 0]
c = len(lst2)
print(c)
```

Output

```
3
```

(j) Write a program to convert a list of tuples

[(10, 20, 30), (150.55, 145.60, 157.65), ('A1', 'B1', 'C1')]

into a list

[(10, 150.55, 'A1'), (20, 145.60, 'B1'), (30, 157.65, 'C1')]

Program

```
lst = [(10, 20, 30), (150.55, 145.60, 157.65), ('A1', 'B1', 'C1')]
lst1 = [ ]
for a, b, c in zip(*lst) :
    lst1.append((a, b, c))
print(lst1)
```

Output

[(10, 150.55, 'A1'), (20, 145.6, 'B1'), (30, 157.65, 'C1')]

(k)   What will be the output of the following program:

```
x = [[1, 2, 3, 4], [4, 5, 6, 7]]
y = [[1, 1], [2, 2], [3, 3], [4, 4]]
l1 = [xrow for xrow in x]
print(l1)
l2 = [(xrow, ycol) for ycol in zip(*y) for xrow in x]
print(l2)
```

Output

[[1, 2, 3, 4], [4, 5, 6, 7]]
[([1, 2, 3, 4], (1, 2, 3, 4)), ([4, 5, 6, 7], (1, 2, 3, 4)), ([1, 2, 3, 4], (1, 2, 3, 4)), ([4, 5, 6, 7], (1, 2, 3, 4))]

(l)   Write a program that uses a generator to create a set of unique words from a line input through the keyboard.

Program

```
line = input('Enter a sentence: ')
s = set(line.split( ))
print(s)
```

Output

```
Enter a sentence: I did not do this. He did it or she did it
{'it', 'or', 'do', 'He', 'she', 'did', 'this.', 'I', 'not'}
```

(m) Write a program that uses a generator to find out maximum marks obtained by a student and his name from tuples of multiple students.

Program

```
def getname(stud, mm) :
    if stud[1] == mm :
        return stud[0]

lst = [('Ajay', 45), ('Sujay', 55), ('Nirmal', 40), ('Vijay', 75)]
```

```
maxmarks = max(student[1] for student in lst)
for student in lst :
    name = getname(student, maxmarks)
print(name, maxmarks )
```

Output

Vijay 75

(n) Write a program that uses a generator that generates characters from a string in reverse order.

Program

```
n = 'Sacchidanand'
revn = [ch for ch in n[::-1]]
print(revn)
```

Output

['d', 'n', 'a', 'n', 'a', 'd', 'i', 'h', 'c', 'c', 'a', 'S']

(o) What is the difference between the following statements:

```
sum([x**2 for x in range(20)])
sum(x**2 for x in range(20))
```

Answer

The first expression first generates a list and then obtains the sum of all elements in the list.

The second expression keeps a running sum of square of each number generates as and when they get generated.

Both will yield same result, but the second one is more efficient as it occupies less space.

(p) Suppose there are two lists, each holding 5 strings. Write a program to generate a list that consists of strings that are concatenated by picking corresponding elements from the two lists.

Program

```
lst1 = ['Cat', 'Dog', 'Lion', 'Tiger']
```

```
lst2 = ['Lily', 'Rose', 'Hibiscus', 'Lavender']
lst3 = [(x + y) for x, y in zip(lst1, lst2)]
print(lst3)
```

Output

```
['CatLily', 'DogRose', 'LionHibiscus', 'TigerLavender']
```

(q) 36 unique combinations can result from use of two dice. Create a dictionary which stores these combinations as tuples.

Program

```
lst = [(d1, d2) for d1 in range(1,7) for d2 in range(1,7)]
print(lst)
```

Output

```
[(1, 1), (1, 2), (1, 3), (1, 4), (1, 5), (1, 6), (2, 1), (2, 2), (2, 3), (2, 4), (2,
5), (2, 6), (3, 1), (3, 2), (3, 3), (3, 4), (3, 5), (3, 6), (4, 1), (4, 2), (4, 3),
(4, 4), (4, 5), (4, 6), (5, 1), (5, 2), (5, 3), (5, 4), (5, 5), (5, 6), (6, 1), (6,
2), (6, 3), (6, 4), (6, 5), (6, 6)]
```

21 Exception Handling

[A] State whether the following statements are True or False:

(a) The exception handling mechanism is supposed to handle compile time errors.

Answer

False

(b) It is necessary to declare the exception class within the class in which an exception is going to be thrown.

Answer

False

(c) Every raised exception must be caught.

Answer

True

(d) For one **try** block there can be multiple **except** blocks.

Answer

True

(e) When an exception is raised, an exception class's constructor gets called.

Answer

True

(f) **try** blocks cannot be nested.

Answer

False

(g) Proper destruction of an object is guaranteed by exception handling mechanism.

Answer

False

(h) All exceptions occur at runtime.

Answer

True

(i) Exceptions offer an object-oriented way of handling runtime errors.

Answer

True

(j) If an exception occurs, then the program terminates abruptly without getting any chance to recover from the exception.

Answer

False

(k) No matter whether an exception occurs or not, the statements in the **finally** clause (if present) will get executed.

Answer

True

(l) A program can contain multiple **finally** clauses.

Answer

False

(m) **finally** clause is used to perform cleanup operations like closing the network/database connections.

Answer

True

(n) While raising a user-defined exception, multiple values can be set in the exception object.

Answer

True

(o) In one function/method, there can be only one **try** block.

Answer

False

(p) An exception must be caught in the same function/method in which it is raised.

Answer

False

(q) All values set up in the exception object are available in the **except** block that catches the exception.

Answer

True

(r) If our program does not catch an exception then Python runtime catches it.

Answer

True

(s) It is possible to create user-defined exceptions.

Answer

True

(t) All types of exceptions can be caught using the **Exception** class.

Answer

True

(u) For every **try** block there must be a corresponding **finally** block.

Answer

False

[B] Answer the following:

(a) If we do not catch the exception thrown at runtime then who catches it?

Answer

If we do not catch the exception thrown at runtime then Python runtime catches it.

(b) Explain in short most compelling reasons for using exception handling over conventional error handling approaches.

Answer

Given below are the reasons for preferring exception handling over conventional error handling:

- It allows separation of program's logic from error handling logic making it more reliable and maintainable.

- Propagation of exception information from the place where an exception occurred to the place where it is tackled is done by runtime environment and is not the programmer's responsibility.

- It allows guaranteed cleanup in event of runtime errors.

(c) Is it necessary that all classes that can be used to represent exceptions be derived from base class **Exception**?

Answer

Yes

(d) What is the use of a **finally** block in Python exception handling mechanism?

Answer

Cleanup activities like releasing external resources, network connections or database connections etc. is done in the finally block since it gets called irrespective of whether an exception occurred or not.

(e) How does nested exception handling work in Python?

Answer

If an exception is raised in the nested try block, the nested except block is used to handle it. If it does not then the outer except blocks are used to handle the exception.

(f) Write a program that receives 10 integers and stores them and their cubes in a dictionary. If the number entered is less than 3, raise a user-defined exception **NumberTooSmall**, and if the number entered is more than 30, then raise a user-defined exception **NumberTooBig**. Whether an exception occurs or not, at the end print the contents of the dictionary.

Program

```python
class NumberTooSmall(Exception) :
  def __init__(self, num) :
    self.num = num

  def get_details(self) :
    return {'Number too small' : self.num}

class NumberTooBig(Exception) :
  def __init__(self, num) :
    self.num = num

  def get_details(self) :
    return {'Number too big' : self.num}

class Numbers :
  def __init__(self) :
    self.dct = { }

  def append(self, num, cube ) :
```

```python
        self.dct[num] = cube

    def display(self) :
        for k, v in self.dct.items( ) :
            print(k, v)
        print( )

n = Numbers( )
print('Enter 10 numbers between 3 to 30 :')
try :
    for x in range(10) :
        num = int(input( ))
        if num > 30 :
            raise NumberTooBig(num)
        elif num < 3 :
            raise NumberTooSmall(num)
        else :
            cube = num * num *num
            n.append(num, cube)
except NumberTooBig as ntb :
    print(ntb.get_details( ))
except NumberTooSmall as nts :
    print(nts.get_details( ))
finally :
    n.display( )
```

Output

```
Enter 10 numbers between 3 to 30 :
5
6
8
9
12
10
2
{'Number too small': 2}
5 125
6 216
8 512
9 729
12 1728
```

10 1000

(g) What's wrong with the following code snippet?

```
try :
    # some statements
except :
    # report error 1
except ZeroDivisionError :
    # report error 2
```

Answer

Empty except block must be the last except block.

(h) Which of these keywords is not part of Python's exception handling—**try, catch, throw, except, raise, finally, else**?

Answer

catch and **throw** are not part of Python's exception handling.

(i) What will be the output of the following code?

```
def fun( ) :
    try :
        return 10
    finally :
        return 20

k = fun( )
print(k)
```

Output

20

22

File Input/Output

[A] State whether the following statements are True or False:

(a) If a file is opened for reading, it is necessary that the file must exist.

Answer

True

(b) If a file opened for writing already exists, its contents would be overwritten.

Answer

True

(c) For opening a file in append mode it is necessary that the file should exist.

Answer

False

[B] Answer the following:

(a) On opening a file for reading which of the following activities are performed:

1. The disk is searched for existence of the file.
2. The file is brought into memory.
3. A pointer is set up which points to the first character in the file.
4. All the above.

Answer

All the above.

(b) Is it necessary that a file created in text mode must always be opened in text mode for subsequent operations?

Answer

Yes

(c) While using the statement,

fp = open('myfile', 'r')

what happens if,

- 'myfile' does not exist on the disk
- 'myfile' exists on the disk

Answer

The disk is searched for existence of the 'myfile'. If it doesn't exist then **FileNotFoundError** exception is raised. If it exists it is brought into memory and a pointer is set up which points to the first character in the file.

(d)   While using the statement,

f = open('myfile', 'wb')

what happens if,

- 'myfile' does not exist on the disk
- 'myfile' exists on the disk

Answer

The disk is searched for existence of the 'myfile'. If it doesn't exist then **FileNotFoundError** exception is raised. If it exists it is brought into memory and a pointer is set up which points to the first byte in the file.

(e)   A floating-point list contains percentage marks obtained by students in an examination. To store these marks in a file 'marks.dat', in which mode would you open the file and why?

Program

'marks.dat' should be opened in 'wb' mode. This is because in binary mode when we store a number in a disk file, it occupies as many bytes as it occupied in memory. If file is opened in 'w' mode then the number is stored character by character and hence would occupy as many bytes as the length of the number.

[C]   Attempt the following:

(a)   Write a program to read a file and display its contents along with line numbers before each line.

Program

```
# Display file contents
f = open('sample.txt', 'r')
while True :
   data = f.readline( )
   if data == '' :
      break
   print(data)
f.close( )
```

Output

CPython - is the reference implementation, written in C.
PyPy - Written in a subset of Python language called RPython.
Jython - Written in Java.
IronPython - Written in C#.

(b) Write a program to append the contents of one file at the end of another.

Program

```
# Append files
f1 = open('sample.txt', 'r')
para1 = ''
while True :
   data = f1.readline( )
   if data == '' :
      break
   para1 += data

f2 = open('trial.txt', 'r+')
para2 = ''
while True :
   data = f2.readline( )
   if data == '' :
      break
   para2 += data

para2 += para1
print(para2)
```

```
f2.seek(0, 0)
f2.write(para2)
f1.close( )
f2.close( )
```

Output

'sample.txt' contains a few lines in lower case. 'trial.txt. contains the same lines in uppercase. After concatenation the contents of 'tiral.txt' is as shown below:

```
CPYTHON - IS THE REFERENCE IMPLEMENTATION, WRITTEN IN C.
PYPY - WRITTEN IN A SUBSET OF PYTHON LANGUAGE CALLED RPYTHON.
JYTHON - WRITTEN IN JAVA.
IRONPYTHON - WRITTEN IN C#.
CPython - is the reference implementation, written in C.
PyPy - Written in a subset of Python language called RPython.
Jython - Written in Java.
IronPython - Written in C#.
```

(c) Suppose a file contains student's records with each record containing name and age of a student. Write a program to read these records and display them in sorted order by name.

Program

```
# Sort records in a file
import operator
f = open('students.txt', 'r')
dct = { }
while True :
    data = f.readline( )
    if data == '' :
        break
    stud = data.split( )
    dct[stud[0]] = stud[1]

f.close( )
lst = sorted(dct.items( ), key = operator.itemgetter(0))
for item in lst :
    print(item[0], item[1])
```

Output

```
Anil 23
Prabhu 22
Rakesh 25
Sameer 30
Sanjay 25
Suresh 33
```

(d) Write a program to copy contents of one file to another. While doing so replace all lowercase characters with their equivalent uppercase characters.

Program

```
# Convert file contents to uppercase
f1 = open('stud1.txt', 'r')
f2 = open('stud2.txt', 'w')
while True :
    data = f1.readline( )
    if data == '' :
        break
    data = data.upper( )
    f2.write(data)

f1.close( )
f2.close( )
```

Output

```
SANJAY 25
SAMEER 30
ANIL 23
SURESH 33
PRABHU 22
RAKESH 25
```

(e) Write a program that merges lines alternately from two files and writes the results to new file. If one file has less number of lines than the other, the remaining lines from the larger file should be simply copied into the target file.

Program

```
# Merge two files alternating its lines
f1 = open('sample.txt', 'r')
f2 = open('trial.txt', 'r')
f3 = open('combined.txt', 'w')
while True :
    data1 = f1.readline( )
    if data1 == '' :
        break
    f3.write(data1)
    data2 = f2.readline( )
    if data2 == '' :
        break
    f3.write(data2)

if data1 != '' :
    while True :
        data1 = f1.readline( )
        if data1 == '' :
            break
        f3.write(data1)

if data2 != '' :
    while True :
        data2 = f2.readline( )
        if data2 == '' :
            break
        f3.write(data2)

f1.close( )
f2.close( )
f3.close( )
```

Output

File 'sample.txt' contains following lines:

1. SANJAY 25
2. SAMEER 30
3. ANIL 23
4. SURESH 33
5. PRABHU 22

6. DINESH 40
7. Suresh 34

File 'trial.txt' contains following lines:

1. Sandhya 25
2. Seema 30
3. Swati 23
4. Supriya 33
5. Sunidhi 22

Resulting file 'comined.txt' contains following lines:

1. SANJAY 25
1. Sandhya 25
2. SAMEER 30
2. Seema 30
3. ANIL 23
3. Swati 23
4. SURESH 33
4. Supriya 33
5. PRABHU 22
5. Sunidhi 22
6. DINESH 40
7. Suresh 34

(f)   Write a program to encrypt/decrypt a file using:

(1)   Offset cipher: In this cipher each character from the source file is offset with a fixed value and then written to the target file.

For example, if character read from the source file is 'A', then write a character represented by 'A' + 128 to the target file.

(2)   Substitution cipher: In this cipher each for character read from the source file a corresponding predetermined character is written to the target file.

For example, if character 'A' is read from the source file, then a '!' would be written to the target file. Similarly, every 'B' would be substituted by '5' and so on.

Program

```
# Offset cipher
def encrypt(f1, f2) :
```

```python
    data = f1.read( )
    for ch in data :
      f2.write((chr(ord(ch) + 128)))

def decrypt(f1, f2) :
    data = f1.read( )
    for ch in data :
      f2.write((chr(ord(ch) - 128)))


source = input('Enter source file name: ')
target = input('Enter target file name: ')
f1 = open(source, 'r', encoding = 'utf-8')
f2 = open(target, 'w', encoding = 'utf-8')
ch = input('Encrypt or Decrypt (E/D)? ')
if ch == 'E' :
    encrypt(f1, f2)
elif ch == 'D' :
    decrypt(f1, f2)
f1.close( )
f2.close( )
```

Output

First run of the program:

```
Enter source file name: sample.txt
Enter target file name: trial.txt
Encrypt or Decrypt (E/D)? E
Encryption complete!
```

Second run of the program:

```
Enter source file name: trial.txt
Enter target file name: sample.txt
Encrypt or Decrypt (E/D)? D
```

Program

```python
# Substitution cipher
def encrypt(f1, f2) :
    s1 = ' `1234567890-=~!@#$%^&*()_+qwertyuiop[]QWERTYUIOP
          {}asdfghjkl;\'ASDFGHJKL:"zxcvbnm,./ZXCVBNM<>?'
    s2 = ' \'ASDFGHJKL:"zxcvbnm,./ZXCVBNM<>?`1234567890-=~!@
          #$%^&*()_+qwertyuiop[]QWERTYUIOP{}asdfghjkl;'
```

```python
    data = f1.read( )
    for ch in data :
      pos = s1.find(ch)
      if pos == -1 :
        f2.write(ch)
      else :
        f2.write(s2[pos])

def decrypt(f1, f2) :
  s1 = ' `1234567890-=~!@#$%^&*()_+qwertyuiop[]QWERTYUIOP
          {}asdfghjkl;\'ASDFGHJKL:"zxcvbnm,./ZXCVBNM<>?'
  s2 = ' \'ASDFGHJKL:"zxcvbnm,./ZXCVBNM<>?`1234567890-=~!@
          #$%^&*()_+qwertyuiop[]QWERTYUIOP{}asdfghjkl;'
  data = f1.read( )
  for ch in data :
    pos = s2.find(ch)
    if pos == -1 :
      f2.write(ch)
    else :
      f2.write(s1[pos])

source = input('Enter source file name: ')
target = input('Enter target file name: ')
f1 = open(source, 'r', encoding = 'utf-8')
f2 = open(target, 'w', encoding = 'utf-8')
ch = input('Encrypt or Decrypt (E/D)? ')
if ch == 'E' :
  encrypt(f1, f2)
elif ch == 'D' :
  decrypt(f1, f2)
f1.close( )
f2.close( )
```

Output

First run of the program:

Enter source file name: sample.txt
Enter target file name: trial.txt
Encrypt or Decrypt (E/D)? E
Encryption complete!

Second run of the program:

```
Enter source file name: trial.txt
Enter target file name: sample.txt
Encrypt or Decrypt (E/D)? D
```

(g) Suppose an Employee object contains following details:

employee code
employee name
date of joining
salary

Write a program to serialize and deserialize this data.

Program

```
# Serialization, Deserialization of employee record
import json
def encode_employee(x):
    if isinstance(x, Employee) :
        return(x.ecode, x.ename, x.doj, x.sal)
    else :
        raise TypeError('Complex object is not JSON serializable')

def decode_employee(dct):
    if '__Employee__' in dct :
        return Employee(dct['ecode'], dct['ename'], dct['doj'], dct['sal'])
    return dct

class Employee :
    def __init__(self, ecode, ename, doj, sal) :
        self.ecode = ecode
        self.ename = ename
        self.doj = doj
        self.sal = sal

    def print_data(self) :
        print(self.ecode, self.ename, self.doj, self.sal)

e = Employee('A101', 'Sameer', '17/11/2017', 25000)
f = open('data', 'w+')
json.dump(e, f, default = encode_employee)
f.seek(0)
```

```
ine = json.load(f, object_hook = decode_employee)
print(ine)
```

Output

```
['A101', 'Sameer', '17/11/2017', 25000]
```

(h) A hospital keeps a file of blood donors in which each record has the format:

Name: 20 Columns
Address: 40 Columns
Age: 2 Columns
Blood Type: 1 Column (Type 1, 2, 3 or 4)

Write a program to read the file and print a list of all blood donors whose age is below 25 and whose blood type is 2.

Program

```
# Formatted reading/writing
donors = {
                'Sanjay' : ['Gokulpeth', 25, 1],
                'Sunil' : ['Shankarnagar', 26, 2],
                'Akash' : ['Sitaburdi', 27, 3],
                'Rahul' : ['Ramnagar', 23, 2],
                'Riddhi' : ['Dharampeth', 22, 2],
                'Mangal' : ['Ramdaspeth', 21, 2]
          }
f = open('donors.txt', 'w+')
for k, v in donors.items( ) :
  s = '{0:20s}{1:40s}{2:2s}{3:1s}\n'.format(k, v[0], str(v[1]), str(v[2]))
  f.write(s)
f.seek(0,0)
while True :
  data = f.readline( )
  if data == '' :
    break
  nam = data[:20]
  address = data[20:59]
  age = int(data[60:62:])
  bloodtype = int(data[62:])
  if age < 25 and bloodtype == 2 :
    print(nam, address, age, bloodtype)
```

f.close( )

Output

Rahul	Ramnagar	23 2
Riddhi	Dharampeth	22 2
Mangal	Ramdaspeth	21 2

(i) Given a list of names of students in a class, write a program to store the names in a file on disk. Make a provision to display the nth name in the list, where **n** is read from the keyboard.

Program

```
# Modify records in a file
names = ['Sanjay', 'Sunil', 'Akash', 'Rahul', 'Riddhi', 'Mangal']
f = open('students.txt', 'w+')
for studname in names :
    f.write(studname + '\n')
num = int(input('Enter student number: '))
f.seek(0,0)
i = 1
while i < num :
    data = f.readline( )
    i += 1

data = f.readline( )
print('Num =', num, 'Name =', data)
f.close( )
```

Output

```
Enter student number: 4
Num = 4 Name = Rahul
```

(j) Assume that a Master file contains two fields, roll number and name of the student. At the end of the year, a set of students join the class and another set leaves. A Transaction file contains the roll numbers and an appropriate code to add or delete a student.

Write a program to create another file that contains the updated list of names and roll numbers. Assume that the Master file and the Transaction file are arranged in ascending order by roll numbers. The updated file should also be in ascending order by roll numbers.

Program

```
# Processing master - transacton files
fm = open('master.txt', 'r')
mdata = fm.readlines( )

ft = open('tran.txt', 'r')
while True :
  trec = ft.readline( )
  if trec == '' :
    break
  tfields = trec.split( )

  if len(tfields) == 2 :
    count = 0
    for record in mdata :
      mfields = record.split( )
      if tfields[0] == mfields[0] :
        break
      count += 1
    del(mdata[count])

  if len(tfields) == 3 :
    mdata.append(tfields[0] + ' ' + tfields[1] + '\n')

sdata = sorted(mdata)
fp = open('processed.txt', 'w')
for item in sdata :
  print(item)
  item = item.split( )
  rec = item[0] + ' ' + item[1] + '\n'
  fp.write(rec)

fm.close( )
ft.close( )
fp.close( )
```

Output

'master.txt' contains following records:

A101 Sanjay

A102 Ajay
A103 Anuja
A104 Akhil
A105 Bhushan
A106 Ankit
A107 Vivek
A108 Ankita
A109 Aditi
A110 Harsha

'tran.txt' contains following records:

A101 D
A105 D
A112 Dheeraj A
A105 Dilip A

'processed.txt' contains following records after additions and deletions:

A102 Ajay
A103 Anuja
A104 Akhil
A105 Dilip
A106 Ankit
A107 Vivek
A108 Ankita
A109 Aditi
A110 Harsha
A112 Dheeraj

(k) Given a text file, write a program to create another text file deleting the words "a", "the", "an" and replacing each one of them with a blank space.

Program

```
# Delete file contents selectively
f = open('a.txt', 'r')
data = f.read( )
f.close( )
data = data.replace(' a ', ' ')
data = data.replace(' an ', ' ')
data = data.replace(' the ', ' ')
```

```
f = open('b.txt', 'w')
f.write(data)
f.close( )
```

Output

The input file 'a.txt' contains following text:

The world is full of duplicates.
I want an apple a day.
I cannot do the stuff that you want me to do.

The output file 'b.txt' contains following text:

The world is full of duplicates.
I want apple day.
I cannot do stuff that you want me to do.

23 Miscellany

[A] State whether the following statements are True or False:

(a) We can send arguments at command-line to any Python program.

Answer

True

(b) The zeroth element of **sys.argv** is always the name of the file being executed.

Answer

True

(c) In Python a function is treated as an object.

Answer

True

(d) A function can be passed to a function and can be returned from a function.

Answer

True

(e) A decorator adds some features to an existing function.

Answer

True

(f) Once a decorator has been created, it can be applied to only one function within the program.

Answer

False

(g) It is mandatory that the function being decorated should not receive any arguments.

Answer

False

(h) It is mandatory that the function being decorated should not return any value.

Answer

False

(i) Type of 'Good!' is bytes.

Answer

False

(j) Type of msg in **msg = 'Good!'** is **str**.

Answer

True

[B] Answer the following:

(a) Is it necessary to mention the docstring for a function immediately below the **def** statement?

Answer

Yes

(b) Write a program using command-line arguments to search for a word in a file and replace it with the specified word. The usage of the program is shown below.

C:\> change -o oldword -n newword -f filename

Program

```
# change.py
import sys
import getopt
sys.argv = ['change.py', '-o', 'Unit', '-n', 'UNIT', '-f', 'Syllabus.txt']
if len(sys.argv) != 7 :
    print('Incorrect usage')
    print('change -o oldword -n newword -f filename')
    sys.exit(1)
```

```
try :
  options, arguments = getopt.getopt(sys.argv[1:],'ho:n:f:')
except getopt.GetoptError :
  print('change -o oldword -n newword -f filename')
else :
  for opt, arg in options :
    if opt == '-h' :
      print('change -o oldword -n newword -f filename')
      sys.exit(2)
    elif opt == '-o' :
      oldword = arg
    elif opt == '-n' :
      newword = arg
    elif opt == '-f' :
      filename = arg
  else :
    print('old word:', oldword)
    print('newword: ', newword)
    print('filename:', filename)
    if oldword and newword and filename:
      f = open(filename, 'r')
      data = f.read( )
      f.close( )
      data = data.replace(oldword, newword)
      f = open(filename, 'w')
      f.write(data)
      f.close( )
```

Tips

The program is stored in the file 'change.py'. The file 'syllabus.txt' is present in the same folder as 'change.py'. It contains the following text:

Unit 1 : Object Oriented Programming
Unit 2 : Data encapsulation
Unit 3 : Inheritance
Unit 4 : Polymorphism
Unit 5 : Late binding
Unit 6 : Constructor
Unit 7 : Method overloading

(c)	Write a program that can be used at command prompt as a calculating utility. The usage of the program is shown below.

C:\> calc <switch> <n> <m>

Where, **n** and **m** are two integer operands. **switch** can be any arithmetic operator. The output should be the result of the operation.

Program

```
import sys
if len(sys.argv) != 4 :
    print('Incorrect usage')
    print('calc operator number number')
    sys.exit(1)

operator = sys.argv[1]
m = int(sys.argv[2])
n = int(sys.argv[3])
if operator == '+' :
    result = m + n
    print('operator =', operator, 'm =', m, 'n =', n, 'result =', result)
elif operator == '-' :
    result = m - n
    print('operator =', operator, 'm =', m, 'n =', n, 'result =', result)
elif operator == '*' :
    result = m * n
    print('operator =', operator, 'm =', m, 'n =', n, 'result =', result)
elif operator == '/' :
    result = m * n
    print('operator =', operator, 'm =', m, 'n =', n, 'result =', result)
else :
    print('Illegal operator')
```

Output

The program can be executed at command-line as shown below:

C:\>ilde -r calc.py + 23 45

On execution is produces the following output:

operator = + m = 23 n = 45 result = 68

(d) Rewrite the following expressions using bitwise compound assignment operators:

```
a = a | 3        a = a & 0x48        b = b ^ 0x22
c = c << 2       d = d >> 4
```

Answer

```
a |= 3           a &= 0x48        b ^= 0x22
c <<= 2          d >>= 4
```

(e) Consider an unsigned integer in which rightmost bit is numbered as 0. Write a function **checkbits(x, p, n)** which returns True if all 'n' bits starting from position 'p' are on, False otherwise. For example, **checkbits(x, 4, 3)** will return true if bits 4, 3 and 2 are 1 in number **x**.

Program

```python
def display_bits(n) :
    for i in range(7, -1, -1) :
        andmask = 1 << i
        k = n & andmask
        print('0', end = '') if k == 0 else print('1', end = '')
    print( )

def checkbits(x, p, n) :
    no = 0
    for i in range(0, n) :
        if ((x >> (p - 1)) & 1) != 1 :
            return 0
        p -= 1
    return 1

num = int(input('Enter a number between 0 to 255: '))
display_bits(num)
p = int(input('Enter position: '))
n = int(input('Enter number of bits: '))
flag = checkbits(num, p, n)
if flag == 1 :
    print(n, 'bits starting from position', p, 'are on')
else :
    print(n, 'bits starting from position', p, 'are off')
```

Output

```
Enter a number between 0 to 255: 255
11111111
Enter position: 4
Enter number of bits: 3
3 bits starting from position 4 are on
Enter a number between 0 to 255: 96
01100000
Enter position: 6
Enter number of bits: 3
3 bits starting from position 6 are off
```

(f)   Write a program to receive a number as input and check whether its 3rd, 6th and 7th bit is on.

Program

```python
# Program to check whether 3rd, 6th and 7th bit of a number is on
def display_bits(n) :
    for i in range(7, -1, -1) :
        andmask = 1 << i
        k = n & andmask
        print('0', end = '') if k == 0 else print('1', end = '')

num = int(input('Enter a number between 0 to 255: '))
display_bits(num)
j = num & 0x08
print( )

print('Its third bit is off') if j == 0 else print('Its third bit is on')
j = num & 0x40
print('Its sixth bit is off') if j == 0 else print('Its sixth bit is on')
j = num & 0x80
print('Its seventh bit is off') if j == 0 else print('Its seventh bit is on')
```

Output

```
Enter a number between 0 to 255: 65
01000001
Its third bit is off
Its sixth bit is on
```

Its seventh bit is off

(g) Write a program to receive a 8-bit number into a variable and then exchange its higher 4 bits with lower 4 bits.

Program

```
# Program to exchange a number's higher 4 bits with lower 4 bits
def display_bits(n) :
    for i in range(7, -1, -1) :
        andmask = 1 << i
        k = n & andmask
        print('0', end = '') if k == 0 else print('1', end = '')

num = int(input('Enter a number between 0 to 255: '))
display_bits(num)
n1 = num << 4
n2 = num >> 4
num = n1 | n2
print('\nAfter exchanging bits:')
display_bits(num)
```

Output

```
Enter a number between 0 to 255: 64
01000000
After exchanging bits:
00000100
```

(h) Write a program to receive a 8-bit number into a variable and then set its odd bits to 1.

Program

```
def display_bits(n) :
    for i in range(7, -1, -1) :
        andmask = 1 << i
        k = n & andmask
        print('0', end = '') if k == 0 else print('1', end = '')

def modify_oddbits(n) :
    for i in range(7, -1, -2) :
        ormask = 1 << i
```

```
        n = n | ormask
    return n

num = int(input('Enter a number between 0 to 255: '))
display_bits(num)
num = modify_oddbits(num)
print( )
display_bits(num)
```

Output

```
Enter a number between 0 to 255: 24
00011000
10111010
```

24

Multi-threading

[A] State whether the following statements are True or False:

(a) Multi-threading improves the speed of execution of the program.

Answer

True

(b) A running task may have several threads running in it.

Answer

True

(c) Multi-processing is same as multi-threading.

Answer

False

(d) If we create a class that inherits from the **Thread** class, we can still inherit our class from some other class.

Answer

True

(e) It is possible to change the name of the running thread.

Answer

True

(f) To launch a thread we must explicitly call the function that is supposed to run in a separate thread.

Answer

False

(g) To launch a thread we must explicitly call the **run( )** method defined in a class that extends the **Thread** class.

Answer

False

(h) Though we do not explicitly call the function that is supposed to run in a separate thread, it is possible to pass arguments to the function.

Answer

True

(i) We cannot control the priority of multiple threads that we may launch in a program.

Answer

False

[B] Answer the following:

(a) What is the difference between multi-processing and multi-threading?

Answer

Multi-processing is the ability to execute multiple processes simultaneously.

Multi-threading is the ability to execute multiple parts (units) of a program simultaneously.

(b) What is the difference between preemptive multi-threading and cooperative multi-threading?

Answer

Preemptive multi-threading - The OS decides when to switch from one task to another.

Cooperative multi-threading - The task decides when to give up the control to the next task.

(c) Which are the two methods available for launching threads in a Python program?

Answer

- By passing a name of the function that should run as a separate thread, to the constructor of the **Thread** class.

- By overriding **__init__( )** and **run( )** methods in a subclass of **Thread** class.

(d) If **Ex** class extends the **Thread** class, then can we launch multiple threads for objects of **Ex** class? If yes, how?

Answer

```
import threading
class Ex(threading.Thread) :
  def __init__(self, s) :
    threading.Thread.__init__(self)
    self.msg = s

  def run(self) :
    while True :
      print(self.msg, end = '\n')

th1 = Ex('Hello')
th1.start( )
th2 = Ex('Hi')
th2.start( )
```

Output

```
HelloHi
HelloHi
HelloHi
HelloHi
HelloHi
HelloHi
HelloHi
... ... ...
```

(e) What do different elements of the following statement signify?

```
th1 = threading.Thread(target = quads, args = (a, b))
```

Answer

threading is a module. It contains a **Thread** class.
Object of **Thread** class is being created here.
The address of the object will get stored in **th1**.

quads is the name of the function that will run in a separate thread.
a, b are the arguments that will be passed to the **quad** function.
The arguments must be in the form of a tuple.

(f)　Write a multithreaded program that copies contents of one folder into another. The source and target folder paths should be input through keyboard.

Program

```python
import sys
import threading
import os
import shutil

def copy_file(input_file, output_file):
    shutil.copyfile(input_file, output_file)
    s = input_file + ' copied!\n'
    print(s)

source = sys.argv[1]
target = sys.argv[2]

if not os.path.exists(source) :
    print('source path does not exist')
    exit( )

if not os.path.exists(target) :
    os.mkdir(target)

os.chdir(source)
lst = os.listdir('.')
tharr = [ ]
for file in lst :
    sourcefilepath = source + '\\' + file
    targetfilepath = target + '\\' + file
    th = threading.Thread(target = copy_file, args = (sourcefilepath, targetfilepath))
    th.start( )
    tharr.append(th)
```

```
for th in tharr :
   th.join( )
```

Output

```
c:\Users\Kanetkar\Desktop\sourcedir\cubes.txt copied!
c:\Users\Kanetkar\Desktop\sourcedir\swam.txt copied!
c:\Users\Kanetkar\Desktop\sourcedir\Resolutions.docx copied!
```

(g) Write a program that reads the contents of 3 files a.txt, b.txt and c.txt sequentially and converts their contents into uppercase and writes them into files aa.txt, bb.txt and cc.txt respectively. The program should report the time required in carrying out this conversion. The files a.txt, b.txt and c.txt should be added to the project and filled with some text. The program should receive the file names as command-line arguments. Suspend the program for 0.5 seconds after reading a line from any file.

Program

```python
import time
import sys
import threading

start_time = time.time( )
lst1= sys.argv[1:4]
lst2 = sys.argv[4:]

if len(lst1) != 3 or len(lst2) != 3 :
   print('Imporper usage')
   print('Correct usage: convert a.txt b.txt c.txt aa.txt bb.txt cc.txt')
   exit( )

for i in range(0, 3) :
   f1 = open(lst1[i], 'r')
   f2 = open(lst2[i], 'w')
   while True :
      data = f1.readline( )
      if data == '' :
         break
      time.sleep(0.5)
      data = data.upper( )
```

```
      f2.write(data)
   f1.close( )
   f2.close( )
end_time = time.time( )
print('Time required = ', end_time - start_time, 'sec')
```

Output

```
Time required =  4.6332080364227295 sec
```

(h) Write a program that accomplishes the same task mentioned in Exercise [B](g) above by launching the conversion operations in 3 different threads.

Program

```
import time
import sys
import threading

def readFile(input_file, output_file):
   f1 = open(input_file, 'r')
   f2 = open(output_file, 'w')
   while True :
      data = f1.readline( )
      if data == '' :
         break
      data = data.upper( )
      f2.write(data)
      time.sleep(0.5)

start_time = time.time( )
lst1= sys.argv[1:4]
lst2 = sys.argv[4:]

if len(lst1) != 3 or len(lst2) != 3 :
   print('Imporper usage')
   print('Correct usage: convert a.txt b.txt c.txt aa.txt bb.txt cc.txt')
   exit( )

tharr = [ ]
for i in range(0, 3) :
```

```
th = threading.Thread(target = readFile, args = (lst1[i], lst2[i]))
th.start( )
tharr.append(th)

for th in tharr:
  th.join( )

end_time = time.time( )
print('Time required = ', end_time - start_time, 'sec')
```

Output

```
Time required =  1.5756025314331055 sec
```

[C] Match the following:

a. Multiprocessing	1. use multiprocessing module
b. Pre-emptive multi-threading	2. use multi-threading
c. Cooperative multi-threading	3. use threading module
d. CPU-bound programs	4. use multi-processing
e. I/O-bound programs	5. use asyncio module

Answer

Multiprocessing - use multiprocessing module
Pre-emptive multi-threading - use threading module
Cooperative multi-threading - use asyncio module
CPU-bound programs - use multi-processing
I/O-bound programs - use multi-threading

25 Synchronization

[A] State whether the following statements are True or False:

(a) All multi-threaded applications should use synchronization.

Answer

False

(b) If 3 threads are going to read from a shared list it is necessary to synchronize their activities.

Answer

False

(c) A Lock acquired by one thread can be released by either the same thread or any other thread running in the application.

Answer

True

(d) If Lock is used in reentrant code then the thread is likely to get blocked during the second call.

Answer

True

(e) Lock and RLock work like a Mutex.

Answer

True

(f) A thread will wait on an Event object unless its internal flag is cleared.

Answer

True

(g) A Condition object internally uses a lock.

Answer

True

(h)   While using RLock we must ensure that we call **release( )** as many times as the number of calls to **acquire( )**.

Answer

True

(i)   Using Lock we can control the maximum number of threads that can access a resource.

Answer

True

(j)   There is no difference between Event and Condition synchronization objects.

Answer

False

[B]   Answer the following:

(a)   Which synchronization mechanisms are used for sharing resources amongst multiple threads?

Answer

Lock, RLock and Semaphore synchronization mechanisms are used for sharing resources amongst multiple threads.

(b)   Which synchronization objects are used for inter-thread communication in a multi-threaded application?

Answer

Event and Condition synchronization objects are used for inter-thread communication in a multi-threaded application.

(c)   What is the difference between a Lock and RLock?

Answer

Lock is used to synchronize access to a shared resource.

Rlock is used to synchronize access to a shared resource in reentrant code.

(d) What is the purpose of the Semaphore synchronization primitive?

Answer

A semaphore is used to limit access to a resource like network connection or a database server to a limited number of threads.

(e) Write a program that has three threads in it. The first thread should produce random numbers in the range 1 to 20, the second thread should display the square of the number generated by first thread on the screen, and the third thread should write cube of number generated by first thread into a file.

Program

```
import threading
import random
import queue
import time
import collections

def generate( ) :
  for i in range(10) :
    cond.acquire( )
    num = random.randrange(10, 20)
    print('Generated number =', num)
    qfors.append(num)
    qforc.append(num)
    cond.notifyAll( )
    cond.release( )

def square( ) :
  for i in range(10) :
    cond.acquire( )
    if len(qfors) :
       num = qfors.popleft( )
       print('num =', num, 'Square =', num * num)
    cond.notifyAll( )
    cond.release( )

def cube( ) :
  for i in range(10) :
    cond.acquire( )
```

```
        if len(qforc) :
          num = qforc.popleft( )
          f.write('num = ' + str(num) + ' cube = ' + str(num * num *
num) + '\n')
        cond.notifyAll( )
        cond.release( )

f = open('cubes.txt', 'w')
qfors = collections.deque( )
qforc = collections.deque( )
cond = threading.Condition( )
th1 = threading.Thread(target = generate)
th2 = threading.Thread(target = square)
th3 = threading.Thread(target = cube)
th1.start( )
th2.start( )
th3.start( )
th1.join ( )
th2.join( )
th3.join( )
f.close( )
print('All Done!!')
```

Output

```
Generated number = 19
Generated number = 12
Generated number = 16
Generated number = 12
Generated number = 11
Generated number = 10
Generated number = 17
Generated number = 10
Generated number = 19
Generated number = 15
num = 19 Square = 361
num = 12 Square = 144
num = 16 Square = 256
num = 12 Square = 144
num = 11 Square = 121
num = 10 Square = 100
num = 17 Square = 289
```

num = 10 Square = 100
num = 19 Square = 361
num = 15 Square = 225
All Done!!

[C] Match the following:

a. RLock	1. limits no. of threads accessing a resource
b. Event	2. useful in sharing resource in reentrant code
c. Semaphore	3. useful for inter-thread communication
d. Condition	4. signals waiting threads on change in state
e. Lock	5. useful in sharing resource among threads

Answer

RLock - useful in sharing resource in reentrant code
Event - useful for inter-thread communication
Semaphore - limits no. of threads accessing a resource
Condition - signals waiting threads on change in state
Lock - useful in sharing resource among threads

9 789389 845013